The Eschatological Judgment of Christ

The Eschatological Judgment of Christ

The Hope of Universal Salvation and the Fear of Eternal Perdition in the Theology of Hans Urs von Balthasar

HENRY C. ANTHONY KARLSON III

PICKWICK *Publications* · Eugene, Oregon

THE ESCHATOLOGICAL JUDGMENT OF CHRIST
The Hope of Universal Salvation and the Fear of Eternal Perdition in the Theology of Hans Urs von Balthasar

Pickwick Publications
An Imprint of Wipf and Stock Publishers
199 W. 8th Ave., Suite 3
Eugene, OR 97401

www.wipfandstock.com

PAPERBACK ISBN: 978-1-4982-9781-3
HARDCOVER ISBN: 978-1-4982-9783-7
EBOOK ISBN: 978-1-4982-9782-0

Cataloguing-in-Publication data:

Names: Karlson, Henry C. Anthony, III, author.

Title: The eschatological judgment of Christ : the hope of universal salvation and the fear of eternal perdition in the theology of Hans Urs von Balthasar / by Henry C. Anthony Karlson III.

Description: Eugene, OR : Pickwick Publications, 2017 | Includes bibliographical references.

Identifiers: ISBN 978-1-4982-9781-3 (paperback) | ISBN 978-1-4982-9783-7 (hardcover) | ISBN 978-1-4982-9782-0 (ebook)

Subjects: LCSH: Balthasar, Hans Urs von, 1905–1988. | Eschatology—History of doctrines—20th century.

Classification: BX4705.B163 K35 2017 (paperback) | BX4705.B163 K35 (ebook)

Manufactured in the U.S.A. 05/17/17

Contents

Acknowledgments

WITH A PROJECT SUCH as this, there are way too many people to thank, so it is way too easy to forget someone who deserves special mention. If I have done so, please forgive me. As such, I would first like to thank all of my friends and family, who have been there as I wrote this, and have, in their own way, given me their support. They know who they are. They do not have to be named.

I would especially like to thank the people who have made sure this book gets finished and in print, including, but not limited to: Doctors Artur Rosman, Sam Rocha, Jennifer Newsome Martin, Tony Annett, and Michael Root. Moreover, I would like to thank the gracious flexibility given to be by the editors at Wipf and Stock, giving me the time to properly complete this project. Finally, I would like to thank my parents, both my mother who is still alive, and my father who has passed away when I was first working on this text; I hope their faith and trust in me has been put to good use.

Abbreviations

DWH	*Dare We Hope "That All Men Be Saved?" With A Short Discourse on Hell.*
ET1, 4	*Explorations in Theology*, vols. 1 and 4
GL1–7	*The Glory of the Lord*, vols. 1–7
HW	*Heart of the World*
KB	*The Theology of Karl Barth*
LA	*Love Alone is Credible*
MP	*Mysterium Paschale*
TD1–5	*Theo-Drama*, vols. 1–5
TL1–3	*Theo-Logic*, vols. 1–3

I

Introduction

PRELIMINARY REMARKS

Hans Urs von Balthasar's eschatology has been greatly misunderstood by many of his critics and supporters alike. While critics recognize that he tried to give nuance to his eschatology, they still tend to portray him as a representative of universalism, albeit a "light" form of universalism. Ralph Martin, in his book, *Will Many Be Saved,* believes that this is the case with Balthasar, saying that Balthasar only stops short of formal acceptance of the theory of *apokakatasis,* that is, formally stating all will be saved.[1] Those who have a natural affinity with such a universalism also perceive him in this fashion, giving ammunition to his critics, because they will say that even those supporters understood Balthasar as a universalist (ignoring those who reject such a portrayal of him).

Sadly, not enough scholarly studies have taken Balthasar seriously when he said that he rejected universalism. The way he addressed the possibility of hell is hardly seen in such presentations, making it seem as if it was ignored by Balthasar, giving support to those who would suggest he was simply a universalist.

1. See Martin, *Will Many Be Saved,* 135. While several critics of Balthasar's theology exist, Martin represents a popular and well-received synthesis of such criticism , allowing it to serve as a representation of what such criticism entails and to see how it often misunderstands Balthasar's eschatology.

Nothing can be further from the truth.

Hell was real for Balthasar. He often made it clear in his writings that hell is something all should fear. There is no pretend with hell. Its reality was proven by the work of Christ. No one's eschatological fate is known until they are judged by Christ. Presumption of perdition but also salvation is not just erroneous, but spiritually dangerous. Christ has provided what everyone needs in order to be saved, giving everyone reason why they can hope for their own salvation. Such salvation is not certain. Sin can still cause someone to be lost for eternity. Christ's grace must be freely accepted for salvation to take effect. Sin, if obstinately held, can turn a sinner away from Christ, and if they perpetually hold on to their sin, they can find themselves stuck in hell, constantly turning away from Christ and his offer of grace.

While there have been a few scholarly works which reflect, at least in part, Balthasar's considerations on eternal perdition, such theological examinations have not been given the reading they deserve. In popular parlance, Balthasar continues to be seen as a universalist. In order for Balthasar's theology to be given adequate consideration, this one-sided approach to his eschatology needs to be rejected and a more comprehensive presentation of his over-arching eschatology needs to be done. This small book intends to help deal with this problem by giving greater emphasis on Balthasar's theology of perdition, showing how it is tied with and intricately connected with his hope that all might be saved. Its main purpose is to provide a better picture of Balthasar's eschatology and to answer some of the simplistic charges aimed at him by his critics. It will focus considerable attention on Balthasar's own words, more than what might otherwise be seen as the norm, because it will help bring together to the reader texts which are otherwise overlooked or not seen in connection to each other, allowing them to come together to highlight Balthasar's theological beliefs. Moreover, through Balthasar, concerns which the modern age has raised over the theology of hell will be addressed, showing that instead of disregarding the notion of hell, it can and should play an important part in contemporary theological exploration; the last section of the book, after exploring Balthasar's theology in depth, will briefly explore the practical application of his opinions to the theological enterprise today as well as show the questions which remain open and are worth asking for future reflection.

Hans Urs von Balthasar can be very difficult to engage. He wrote theology in a reflective, almost meditative fashion, making it hard for someone to pick up a text of his, read a few pages, and then easily state what he believed. His works often read like poetry, providing some of the same difficulty as poetry has for interpreting his meaning. He liked to take a topic and explore it in many different angles, making it difficult to discern which of those angles, if any, he actually held to himself. Readers of his theological works often find themselves lost in this multi-layered approach and end up feeling as if they know less as to what he believed when they finish reading a text than they did before they started reading it. His views are very hard to pin-point. They do not follow the typical categories critics want to use to examine his writings, as the editors of *The Cambridge Companion to Hans Urs von Balthasar* explained, "his positions cannot be easily categorized. Neither liberal nor conservative as those shopworn terms are normally understood, his theology is in fact extremely subtle and learned, so much so that it cannot be aligned with any contemporary trend, but sits uneasily inside *any* school of thought in the history of theology."[2]

Balthasar was "unsystematic" in his approach to systematic questions. He liked to engage mysteries of the faith as paradoxes, and he did not think it was wise to break down a paradox to find some sort of "resolution" behind them. Instead, he ended up presenting the paradox itself, leaving the reader to contemplate it and address it in their own thoughts.[3] An example of this can be found in the way Balthasar reflected upon the implications of the two natures of Christ upon Christ's consciousness:

> From the standpoint of the single consciousness, he is on earth, a limited man under obedience, while in heaven he is the ruler of the world. However, these speculations lead nowhere: their only result is to bring our attention to the striking fashion how deep

2. Moss and Oakes, "Introduction," 2.

3. This goes with the limitations of human language, that there is a lot that it can say, but in the end, there is a lot which will transcend what can be said, and must be left unsaid. While it can point to and grasp something of the truth, there is always something which transcends what can be said, indeed, what humans can understand, as Anne Carpenter related: "There are really two limits to language, one at the creaturely level and the other (a more complex one) at the level of the relationship between God and the world. The first limit refers to the paradoxical fashion in which human beings can grasp being, and yet in grasping being we are still left with an insurmountable mystery. Truth, von Balthasar reminds us, is not simply what we understand, so that mystery is what we do not yet understand. Truth and mystery are instead concomitant qualities; the truth is genuinely mysterious and this is a positive characteristic of truth and not its mere negation. Further, what can be said of worldly truth is more profoundly the case with respect to God. This is the second limit." Carpenter, "Theo-Poetics," 200.

> the mystery of Kenosis lies. Just as the ancient ontic theology was impotent to render credible the idea that the Incarnation was a "complementary factor" added to the immutable divine nature (for Kenosis is not a *harpagamos*, a gain), so too the theology of consciousness—whether in speculative or empirical guise—did not succeed in finding a "third" position from which the interplay of the divine and human consciousness might be surveyed. The *paradox* must be allowed to stand: in the undiminished humanity of Jesus, the whole power and glory of God are made present to us.[4]

Because Balthasar believed that the truth was best presented through such paradoxes, his position which he believed was found in that paradox often seems vague to a typical first-time reader. Often, he would discuss a theological problem from one side of a paradox, and then from the other, without showing how both sides correlate. This can easily lead a reader to think that Balthasar was not making any particular point when he actually was doing so. A reader will have to ask himself or herself, "What is it Balthasar is trying to say? What is it he is affirming or denying?" They will have to search for answers, and even then, they might come out perplexed, feeling as if an answer cannot be found. Balthasar expects a lot from his audience, to be sure, but this aspect of his style, however beautiful it might be, however necessary it might end up being, does get in the way with a reader's comprehension of his theological explanations.

Another difficulty a reader has with Balthasar is that he left behind a large collection of writings.[5] To get a basic understanding of what he believed on a particular issue often requires the reading of several different works. Just reading one text, however significant it might be, is not enough, especially for something as complicated as his understanding of perdition. He did not want to deny traditional theology, he did not want to be considered unorthodox, but he did question how perdition had come to be taught, leading him to explore the concept and establish some rather unusual explanations for it. This can be seen in the topic at hand and how he famously stated that he hoped that all would be saved. He was clear in saying that this hope must be seen only as a possibility. It must not be seen as a necessary conclusion. To make it necessary would remove from free

4. Balthasar, *Mysterium Paschale*, 3. [Henceforth abbreviated as MP].

5. Msgr. Philippe Barbarin counted more than 10,000 pages of material in 48 books and 529 articles. See Barbarin, *Théologie et Sainteté*, 9, 35.

will from humanity, and it is such free will he wanted to preserve, believing with many of his critics it is not something God would override.[6]

The question of perdition was important to Balthasar. Eschatological questions consistently turned up in his writings. His main concern was to present how and why he could hope that all might be saved. Nonetheless, he also made sure he would explain why he could not be sure this would happen. Because of the way important figures in Catholic tradition, such as St. Augustine, have considered the possibility that a large number of people will be damned, it is not surprising that Balthasar had to defend himself from charges of heresy by his critics. His famous work, *Dare We Hope "That All Men Be Saved?"* served as his major answer to his critics whom he believed were misinterpreting his position or the demands of Catholic doctrine.[7]

Despite his hope that none would be lost, it is important to note, as it is a central concern with this work, that he believed that some, or even many, could end up among the damned. It was not his focus, but it was something he would consider, time and time again, often adding nuances to his thought each time he did so. The condition in which such damned would find themselves in was very important to him because it was intricately connected as to why he thought they could end up among the lost, for their condition is the result of their choice, the choice which they made and continue to make when confronted by Christ which allows them to be among the damned.

While exploring Balthasar's eschatological notions, we will have to limit ourselves when addressing his works; many themes, normally discussed by writers on Balthasar, will be regulated to a secondary value or not approached at all, because they have little to no bearing to our concerns here. This work is not an introduction to his theology as a whole, but a presentation of his theology on perdition. Nonetheless, a few brief statements on his early life and his work with Adrienne von Speyr is appropriate, because they help set up how and why he engaged theology as he did.

6. This is why he opposed any "system-building" which would establish the necessary conclusion that all would be saved. This, he believed, was a fault in Barth's writings. See Balthasar, *Dare We Hope That All Men Be Saved*, 44–45. [Henceforth abbreviated as DWH].

7. DWH was written as a response to many of his critics such as Gerhard Hermes, Heribert Schauff, and Johannes Bökmann, who were trying to suggest that he held to heretical notions about the salvation of all. See DWH 16–20.

EARLY YEARS

Balthasar was born on August 12, 1905, in Lucerne, Switzerland. As a child, he was quite the prodigy, interested in a diversity of studies. Much of what he would explore in his theology developed out of his early life experiences. He believed childhood helped explain to us who we are, and if we want to grasp how we come to know ourselves in the world in relation to God, looking back to childhood helps us. A prime example of this is how he understood the smile of a mother and how it affects her child:

> After a mother has smiled at her child for many days and weeks, she finally receives her child's smile in response. She has awakened love in the heart of her child, and as the child awakens to love, it also awakens to knowledge: the initially empty-sense impressions gather meaningfully around the core of the Thou. Knowledge (with its whole complex of intuition and concept) comes into play, because the play of love has already begun beforehand, initiated by the mother, the transcendent.[8]

Balthasar would not have been able to develop his understanding of self-consciousness and being if he had not seen how his own childhood helped shape his theological reflection. Therefore, it should not be surprising that he recognized the role that his family, and especially his mother, had in providing him his Catholic faith and in the discovery of his priestly vocation.[9]

As a youth, he developed a great love for music. It is easy to see how his would influence his thinking. Music provides inspiration and feelings and ideas which are not always easily translated into words. Balthasar did more than listen to music. He actively studied musical theory, and even published a short treatise on it in 1925. Indeed, before he decided take on *Germanistik* ("Germanic studies") for academic studies, he considered having a career in the professional study of music.

His early engagement with music would be useful for him, because it gave him a unique way to engage philosophy and theology. The study of music suggested a "symphonic understanding" of reality. That is, just as a symphony has many complementary, even rival, parts necessary for the whole, and only when the piece is brought together to a proper conclusion can it be interpreted, so he believed truth should be seen as symphonic, with paradoxical, almost contradictory parts, and only when these parts

8. Balthasar, *Love Alone is Credible*, 76. [Henceforth abbreviated as LA].

9. See Henrici, "Hans Urs von Balthasar," 10.

are brought together in a holistic fashion can the fullness of the truth be presented.[10] Symphonies also gave to Balthasar a way to express the eschatological dilemma which he faced: while an audience listens to the production of a new musical piece, they will not be able to predict the ending of the piece, even though the work as a whole is united and in a good symphony the ending is the proper and fitting conclusion to the piece as a whole. Eschatology, likewise, presents an ending which is the perfect ending for the whole of history and yet it is unpredictable in history: the eschaton must be experienced to know it.[11]

Balthasar earned his doctorate in *Germanistik* at the university of Zürich in 1928. Before he finished his dissertation, in the summer of 1927, he felt called to the priesthood. Instead of being a side-step away from God's calling for him, he believed his studies served as the foundation for that call to be fulfilled.[12] This should not be surprising, given that his doctoral dissertation was his first major engagement with eschatological concerns. In it, he wanted to explain the eschatological dispositions found within modern German literature. It would later be expanded and published as a three volume work, his *Apokalypse der deutschen Seele* (*Apocalypse of the German Soul*).[13]

When he felt the call to the priesthood, Balthasar believed he was also called to a particular kind of priesthood, that of a Jesuit, and so he became a Jesuit novice in 1929. Through his Jesuit studies, he would come into contact not only with the works of St. Ignatius of Loyola (which would have a profound influence upon him), but also with the two men who would become mentors to him and help him get through what he felt was an otherwise dull novitiate: Erich Przywara and Henri de Lubac.[14]

10. Balthasar therefore said revelation, which is the ultimate presentation of truth, is also symphonic in its presentation. "In his revelation, God performs a symphony, and it is impossible to say which is richer: the seamless genius of his composition or the polyphonous orchestra of Creation that he has prepared to play it." Balthasar, *Truth is Symphonic*, 8.

11 To further explore this point, see Nichols, *Scattering the Seed*, 8.

12. See Balthasar, *My Work in Retrospect*, 10.

13. The *Apokalypse der deutschen Seele* (1937–39) was published in three volumes, and would eventually be seen by Balthasar as a rather problematic text, although he did think elements of it still had value: "The work was of insufficient maturity—most of the chapters ought to be rewritten—and yet some of it may still be valid," Balthasar, *Our Task*, 37.

14. He felt that theological education based upon the so-called manualist tradition was stifling and dull. Yet, from both Przywara and de Lubac, he had been given access to

After Balthasar was ordained on July 26, 1936, he was sent to Munich in 1937 to work with the journal *Stimmen der Zeit,* which he would do for two years. While in Munich, he would live with his friend and mentor, Przywara, finish his *Apokalypse der deutschen Seele,* and begin work on his scholarly writings on patristic authors. Things would change for him in 1940 when he would become a student chaplain at Basel. It was due to this move that he would meet both Karl Barth and Adrienne von Speyr.[15]

ADRIENNE VON SPEYR

There is no doubt that the person with the greatest influence upon Balthasar's later theology was Adrienne von Speyr.[16] Balthasar recognized this fact. Indeed, he thought his work could only be understood as it relates

---

the kind of theology which inspired him: one which engaged the modern world without rejecting the great theological legacy of the past. While in France, he also developed an interest in French literature, leading him to the work of Paul Claudel. See Block, "Introduction," 2.

15. There is no doubt that his friendship with Karl Barth would influence him and his work, though the relationship between the two and how much of Barth's work influenced Balthasar is hard to discern. Truly Barth's Christo-centrism and interest in aesthetics certainly had some influence upon Balthasar as Stephen Wigley points out. See Wigley, *Balthasar's Trilogy*, 18–21.

On the other hand, Balthasar also tried to influence Barth, to help him see better the way Christ, in his humanity, was at work in creation, affirming the human condition. Balthasar could affirm what he saw in Barth, but he would also see it needed to be "expanded," as D. Stephen Long put it. See Long, *Saving Karl Barth,* 287.

Affirming the freedom given to humanity by God requires such an expansion, lest humanity becomes overwhelmed by the divinity in Christ and in history.

16. This is something critics of Balthasar like to point out. His relationship with Adrienne von Speyr was and remains controversial; it led him, for example, to leave the Jesuits (in 1951) so that he could continue his work with his new mission, their Secular Institute (The Community of St. John). For this reason, as Jacques Servais pointed out, some Jesuits have found his work with Adrienne to be a point of general concern, believing it negatively affected his theology. See Servais, "Balthasar as Interpreter of the Catholic Tradition," 194.

His work with von Speyr certainly caused him "isolation" from other theologians, as David Moss and Edward T. Oakes point out. Cf. Moss and Oakes, "Introduction," 4–5.

Through von Speyr, Balthasar entered a new kind of theological life, an engagement with the mystical dimensions of Christianity, where his theology was to discuss and use von Speyr's mystical experiences. Because of the claim of mystical "revelation," it is not surprising Balthasar's critics would consider Adrienne von Speyr's reflections a weak-spot in Balthasar's theology. For a criticism of Adrienne von Speyr (and a reply to it), see Gardiner and Servais, "Correcting the Deposit of Faith?," 31–45.

to, and is connected with, the work of von Speyr. He wanted the two of them to be seen as working for one common theological mission.[17] Johann Roten agreed with this analysis: "It should be expected that at least where von Balthasar's theological thinking and writing is concerned, a clear and definite distinction could be made between his work and that of Adrienne. But such is not the case. According to von Balthasar himself, there are topics and thematics in his work after 1940 which, in spite of intense studies, did not play any major role before that time."[18] Nonetheless, with this connection between the two, care must be had, and there should be no supposition that any apparently new theological ideas he had after meeting Adrienne came from her alone and were not something he was already developing in his work. Rather, one of the reasons why they were able to form one theological mission was because Adrienne's contributions exemplified the theological intuitions Balthasar had established for himself.[19]

Before she met Balthasar, Adrienne von Speyr had established herself as a physician. She was also married to her second husband, Werner Kaegi (her first husband, Emil Dürr, had died in 1934). When, in 1940, she considered the possibility of becoming Catholic and she asked who she should talk to, she was introduced to Balthasar. Almost immediately, Balthasar saw something special with her. Without any formal theological training, she was able to grasp what he taught with ease. "In the instructions she understood everything immediately, as though she had only—and for how long!—waited to hear exactly what I was saying in order to affirm it. She was baptized on the Feast of All Saints."[20] Soon after her baptism, she began to have intense mystical experiences which Balthasar was often to witness, or, if he was not there, she told him about them.[21] Her baptism let loose a flurry of grace in her:

17. He wrote the book, *Our Task*, to represent this point, that he did not want his work disconnected from that of von Speyr. See Balthasar, *Our Task*, 13.

18. See Roten, "The Two Halves of the Moon," 75–76.

19. In the end, it is difficult, if not impossible, to determine how they influenced each other. Rather we must realize they came together, encouraging each other, learning from each other, helping each other develop their own aspect of their unified theological mission. Thus, as Mathew Sutton stated, it is impossible for us determine the "proportions" of their influence upon each other. See, for example, Sutton, *Heaven Opens*, 2

20. Balthasar, *First Glance at Adrienne von Sepyr*, 31.

21. These experiences did not start at her baptism. She had them throughout her life. For example, she believed that as a young child she had an encounter with St. Ignatius. During Christmas of 1908, she claims he appeared to her as a strange man, asking her to come with him, which at the time she declined, although she was somewhat interested

> Immediately after her conversion, a veritable cataract of mystical graces poured over Adrienne in a seemingly chaotic storm that whirled her in all directions at once. Graces in prayer above all: she was transported beyond all vocal prayer or self-directed meditation upon God in order to set down somewhere after an indefinite time with new understanding, new love and new resolutions.[22]

Starting in 1941, and occurring every Easter after that, she appeared to experience the passion of Christ. This happened both physically, where she would have stigmata appear on her body, and mentally, where she seemed to have in her consciousness the experience of what Christ felt as he was put on the cross, descended into the realm of the dead, and finally resurrected in glory:

> These passions were not so much a vision of the historical scenes of the suffering that had taken place in Jerusalem—there were only occasional glimpses of these, as if for clarification—rather, they were an experience of the interior sufferings of Jesus in all their fullness and diversity—whole maps of suffering were filled in precisely there where no more than a blank space or a vague idea seemed to exist.[23]

Balthasar would record her experiences, taking great concern to note exactly what she said, treating her words as an important revelations, so that much of what she said during these experiences would be used in Balthasar's later theological work.[24] Indeed, sometimes Balthasar would give the impression that his work was the theological exposition of Adrienne's mystical experiences.[25] Clearly, this is a difficult aspect of Balthasar's thought to accept—that is, the fact that he took so much from Adrienne's mystical experiences and used them as a primary source for his writings. While what he said using them was credible, this does not mean her experiences need go unquestioned. Despite his objections to the contrary, the way he used her experiences differs from those experiences themselves. He

---

and inclined to do so. She would later encounter him again and recognize him as St. Ignatius. See Speyr, *My Early Years*, 32–34.

22. Balthasar, *First Glance*, 33.

23. Ibid., 35.

24. See Nichols, *Divine Fruitfulness*, 114, 116–21.

25. He saw Adrienne von Speyr's experiences as revelation which needed to be applied to theology. He believed his theological studies allowed him to do this, to bring what she had to say to Christian theology. See Sutton, "Hans Urs von Balthasar and Adrienne von Speyr's Ecclesial Relationship," 54–55.

provided to them a systematic framework which interpreted them in an orthodox manner. Reading them outside of that framework, it is possible come to different, indeed possibly dangerous, conclusions from what she said.

Most of the writings of Adrienne von Speyr have Balthasar as their editor. Texts which reveal her mystical experiences, such as her *Book of All Saints*, have Balthasar's helping hand, ready to guide the reader. Her experience of the passion of Christ played an important part of Balthasar's own understanding of Christ's death and its relationship to hell, and this is something he commented upon in his introduction to her *Book of All Saints*, presenting it as a major theme of her writings as a whole:

> Christ visits the kingdom of the damned, which is a mystery that belongs to the Father (as Creator of human freedom and the world's judge), as one who is himself dead; he can be led into this kingdom only as one who has died, who has in obedience to the Father entered into the furthest extremity of Godforsakenness. But hell is the world's "second chaos" (The Creator bought order to the first), which arose through sin and henceforth can be separated from sinners through the Cross of Christ.[26]

Adrienne's experiences would become so mixed into Balthasar's writings that in some of his later works, he would freely quote from her experiences as if she were writing his book for him. That they often took on the notion of Christ's experience with the dead and the revelation of hell, Balthasar leaves his reader no option but to seek after and study Adrienne von Speyr's texts if they want to engage his own works properly.

In Adrienne's writings, there are many themes, while important in and of themselves, which add little to value to a study of Balthasar's understanding eternal perdition, while others cannot be ignored.[27] Among them, one

26. Speyr, *Book of All Saints*, 14.

27. Johann Roten in his essay on Adrienne von Speyr's influences on Balthasar presented twelve themes of Adrienne von Speyr which directly impacted Balthasar's theology: 1) her experience of the passion, 2) a "Johannine" notion of truth, 3) a theology of the Christian states of life, 4) a theology of mission, 5) a way to interpret history through the centering of history in Christ (though this can be disputed, based upon Balthasar's earlier work), 6) a kind of "Catholic universalism" which is more open to the world (again, this was already inherent in Balthasar's theological engagement), 7) the unity of theology and holiness, 8) the relationship between prayer and God's work on the human person, 9) reawakening the Johannine "notion of glory," 10) mission as it relates to the confrontation of "finite and infinite freedom," 11) notions about the office of the priest, and 12) the notion of obedience and its importance in understanding the work of Christ. See Roten, "Marian Anthropological Dimensions," 76–78.

of the most important comes from her understanding of the incarnation, which was intricately connected with Balthasar's own Christology. She began with a rather simple claim: the Divine Son was sent on a mission by the God the Father to save the world. The Son accomplished this difficult task out of loving obedience to the Father.[28] The Son's obedience to the Father presents to humanity the proper way we should respond to God. It is important to note that the Son's obedience was accomplished by his great love: the Son had such love that he willingly "emptied" himself (in *kenosis*) to become man and experience all that humanity experienced. The kenotic act had to be total: he had to completely "empty" himself, and hold nothing back. This was accomplished by his death and descent into hell.

She taught that in his humanity, the Divine Son had taken on all that is human, including human ignorance, so that he could prove his perfect love to the Father. By doing everything he was expected to do, by suffering as he was expected to suffer without complaint, without knowledge of how it would end, Adrienne understood that he proved his love and devotion to the Father: "The hour of the Cross is the hour of the Father; for it is the hour that he alone knows. The Son, who could know it, forgoes that knowledge. One of the reasons the Father has reserved this knowledge for himself surely lies in the fact that the Son's obedience is to undergo the most severe testing possible."[29] Indeed, "His achievement is not merely to suffer the Cross but to endure the suffering of the Cross in the form of obedience the Father has determined."[30]

His death on the cross was not the end of his kenosis; he had to endure in full what the rest of humanity faces in death. In his descent into the grave, he took on himself the full burden of sin, allowing sin to be revealed in and through its effects on him. The burden was pressed upon him with the imposition of the crown of thorns. "He commits no sin, but when the crown of thorns is pressed on his head, he welcomes sins as his own property into himself, without his pure spirit losing anything of its purity."[31] On the cross,

28. Her mystical experience provided what can be seen as a rather psychological understanding of the accomplishment of Christ: she experienced, as it were, some of the feelings and thoughts of Christ. The love the Son has for the Father allows Jesus to follow his mission to its completion, and what Adrienne von Speyr thought she experienced indicates the greatness of his accomplishment. See Sutton, *Heaven Opens*, 147–88 for a thorough presentation of her understanding of Christ's obedience to the Father.

29. Speyr, *The Countenance of the Father*, 71.

30. Ibid., 74.

31. Speyr, *The Passion From Within*, 147.

he experienced being forsaken by the Father, but it was in hell, in the chaos of sin and death, in solidarity with the rest of humanity, he experienced to the very end the Godforsakenness which is brought about by sin. While in hell, Christ suffered as one of the dead, as one who had been forsaken by God; he was not there as a triumphant hero. It was only by such a complete letting go of himself that a new trajectory for death could be created: Christ was brought back to life in the midst of death, reconfiguring the value and meaning of death itself.

Christ's work in hell would have an implication for sinners: through it sin could be removed and the sinner cleansed, with Jesus casting all sin loaded upon him off in the realm of the dead: "As a result of this, evil too is changed in character. It is what is separated, alien, turned away from eternity."[32] Sinners find that the forgiveness of sins is possible in and through the accomplishment of Christ on the cross:

> Evil is seen in its true colors on the Cross, where the Lord bears all sin. On the Cross it was vanquished—not just once, but continuously: because the absolution instituted by the Son to demonstrate the triumphant power of the Cross can be imparted anew every day, because the sinner can always find access to the Lord through the Church, and to the Father through the Lord.[33]

The nature of sin has been changed. "The sin has become a purely objective entity, free from the evaluation and feeling of human consciousness, empty of and free from the subject that committed it."[34] Sin had become objectified, allowing it to be separated from the sinner. In his resurrection Christ is said to have left behind in hell the effigies of sinners, effigies made out their objectified sin.[35]

Since Christ was raised out of the realm of death, sinners can also rise out of death if they join themselves to him. His death was a work of universal love. He loved all the sinners of the world, even as he loved the Father. The resurrection was the Father's confirmation of Christ's love, his affirmation of the Son and his love for humanity. Christ's solidarity with sinners brought the change necessary for the our salvation: "But now the one who has died is he who had freely entered into his death out of love

32. Speyr, *The Gates of Eternal Life*, 112.
33. Ibid., 112–13.
34. Speyr, *Confession*, 54.
35. See Lösel, "A Plain Account of Christian Salvation," 152.

for sinners; and regarding that death the sinner knows that the Father has taken it up and transformed it into everlasting life."[36]

Connected to the incarnation was the work of Jesus' mother, the Virgin Mary. She represented the human reflection of the principle of self-giving love, exactly as the Son did in the divinity, and so offered us an exemplar of how we are to act and react with God. She shows that if someone would completely surrender themselves to God, they would find true freedom in and with God. "The great mystery of the Lord's Mother is the mystery of surrender. It is a surrender that belongs totally to the triune God: to the Father, who gives her her Son; to the Spirit, who overshadows her; and to the Son, who allows himself to be carried by her."[37] Mary had a special mission in the world: she was to represent the whole of humanity with her yes at the annunciation, done so in full obedience to God without anything limiting her from making that yes.[38]

Mary gave herself over to total obedience with God because she loved him. It was a perfect love which manifested itself in the production of the perfect fruit, Jesus Christ. The incarnation was the fulfillment of her yes to God. The incarnation incorporated human freedom into itself by accepting her total devotion and love to God. It was through her yes that the Son was able to take on human nature and represent humanity to the Father. Similarly, he was able to take her yes and unite it with every other human yes to God, and present it to heaven. "Every Yes uttered by man to the Son is laid up there. The Mother's Yes paved a broad road to heaven, so broad that no believer can miss it, but can follow the trail to the Son, to where he can exchange his perishable time for the eternal time of the triune God."[39] Her yes made it possible once and for all for everyone else to say yes to God.

While her yes was made at the annunciation, Mary lived that yes throughout her entire life; she was the open to God, selflessly giving herself to him, doing whatever she was asked:

> Mary knew only from the moment of the Son's conception on that her body was in such a continuity of service. [. . .] She understood that there was nothing in her body, whether hand or face or any other member, that belonged to herself, because everything was

36. Speyr, *The Countenance of the Father*, 87.

37. Speyr, *The Mystery of Death*, 115.

38. See Nichols, *Divine Fruitfulness*, 119, for a beautiful rendition of the *fiat* of Mary as presented by Balthasar and von Speyr.

39. Speyr, *The Gates of Eternal Life*, 138–39.

> harnessed into an uninterrupted service of the Father, of the Son, and of the Holy Spirit.[40]

Adrienne provided two outstanding examples of obedience for Christians to consider and follow: the Son's obedience to the Father and Mary's obedience to God. The two come together to show what the Christian life is about. Each, moreover, demonstrates the contours of that obedience, where Christians are not to expect it would lead them to some earthly glory. If they follow the path of loving obedience, even if it brings them much pain and suffering in their temporal existence, Christians will find their lives affirmed by the Father and what they have done was truly for God's greater glory.

Obedience is possible only in and through grace. Adrienne von Speyr was not a Pelagian. Salvation comes from Christ, not our works: "If we were capable of saving ourselves by our works, this would mean that we were in possession of a power that, applied rightly, would be sufficient to put us in contact with God and to reconcile us to him. The way to God would then be no longer the Son but our ego."[41] The Son's obedience led to a reconfiguration of the world through his death and resurrection, and this change in the world served as the foundation by which humanity can now obey God. When someone says yes to God and obeys him, what they do for him is not to be seen as slavery, for slavery is of sin, but as their loving response to God's grace.[42] Thus, as Andrew Louth put it, the structure of Adrienne's teaching on the Christian life are Marian.[43] Mary shows humanity that it is called to a loving obedience to God which, if followed, will give to them their own fruitful reward. Obedience requires self-giving; the fruit of that sacrifice is the new life given to the Christian by the Spirit thanks to the divesting of the Spirit by Christ.[44]

40. Speyr, *The Letter to the Ephesians,* 37.

41. Ibid., 90–91.

42. Everyone must discern what call God is giving to then, and then decide if they are going to answer it with a yes. If they do, then they properly accepted their ecclesial vocation. See Speyr, *The Christian State of Life,* for her examination of how Christians are to prepare for that call, how they can make the choice to accept it, and the consequences of that choice has upon them once it has been made.

43. See Louth, "The Place of Heart of the World," 149.

44. See Speyr, *The Cross & Sacrament,* 62. This Marian dimension of Adrienne's theology finds its complement in the works of Balthasar and connects with his ecclesiology, as Stephen Lösel noted: "For von Balthasar, Mary functions furthermore as the real-symbol for the mystical person of the church and of all individual believers. [. . .] Through her

The way his encounter with Adrienne quickly influenced Balthasar can be seen by the way he made time to be with her and to record her mystical experiences, but more importantly, through what he wrote after his encounter with her. In 1944, he published *Heart of the World,* his first major theological work. In it, he had already begun to incorporate Adrienne's theology with his own, showing that his major theological writings reflected the theological ideas and notions which he shared with Adrienne von Speyr from the very beginning of his theological writing career.[45] After *Heart of the World*, the rest of his theological work can be seen as a continuous response to his meeting with Adrienne von Speyr, where he worked out the implications of what he learned from her, combining it with the theological knowledge he had gained from his earlier studies.[46]

LATER WORK AND DEATH

Balthasar wrote a significant number of works which must be explored if his understanding of perdition is to be properly presented. Without question his greatest work was his so-called Theological Trilogy, with the first volume of it being published in 1961.[47] This would be the beginning of his

passive acceptance of her Son's suffering and death on the cross, Mary recognizes on behalf of the church that Jesus' sacrifice has taken place for all of humankind. In fact, Mary's consent becomes itself 'a constituent part of his sacrifice,' not equal in importance, yet necessary in its sheer acceptance of what God works on our behalf." Lösel, "Conciliar, not Conciliatory," 33. While both Mary and the church have great importance in the works of Balthasar, we will not be exploring either in depth in our present study. Rather, it is to be understood that when we discuss loving obedience in Balthasar, this Marian dimension, found in the works of Adrienne von Speyr, is a part of what lies behind Balthasar's thoughts.

45. See Louth, "The Place of Heart of the World," 148.

46. Of this relationship, Balthasar once told Angelo Scola, "Adrienne is a world. Not only has she built up a world community, but built it upon an extensive theology, which in its substance derives from her. All I attempted to do was gather it up and embed it in a space, such as the theology of the Fathers, that of the Middle Ages and the modern age, with which I was fairly familiar. My contribution consisted in providing a comprehensive theological horizon, so that all that was new and valid in her thought would not be watered down or falsified, but be given space to unfold." Balthasar, *Test Everything*, 88.

47. His trilogy was intended as an engagement of the three transcendentals (beauty, goodness, and truth) for the sake of theology; he went about them in this order to show how he believed humans normally engage these three aspects of being, and how that order should then affect theological reflection of God's revelation. One is attracted to God through beauty, and then they are called to engage God (following the question of what

most sophisticated stage of writing, and that Trilogy would, for the most part, be the central focus of his later theological reflections. In 1967, Adrienne von Speyr died. She left Balthasar with a large collection of transcriptions to edit and publish. He would do so as he wrote his own theological works, often combing both tasks together. This can be seen in *Mysterium Paschale* (1969), his single-volume work on the death and resurrection of Christ. In it he gave a focused explanation of his theology Christ's descent into hell, revealing how much he had made Adrienne's theological views his own.[48] It was a major work in and of itself, causing quite a theological stir, but Balthasar did not feel it dealt with the question of Holy Saturday sufficiently. He would take up the issues in *Mysterium Paschale,* and deal with them in a more sophisticated manner in the fourth volume of the *Theo-Drama,* published in 1980.[49] He would present his great work of eschatology, the fifth and last volume of his *Theo-Drama,* in 1983.

As Balthasar's eschatological notions were published, critics began to question his ideas, reading his eschatology as if he said hell was empty. This led to the controversy which would remain with him throughout his remaining years, where he would try to explain why he hoped all would be saved even if he did not know if this would happen. Three significant essays came out of this controversy: "Dare We Hope That All Men Be Saved?" (1986), "A Short Discourse on Hell" (1987) and "Apokatastasis" (1988). While defending his beliefs, he continued to write for his trilogy, completing it with the *Epilogue* in 1987.

As a way of showing his respect for Balthasar's theological contributions, Pope John Paul II decided to invest a cardinalship on Balthasar. Balthasar was hesitant to accept it, but when he did, he humbly prepared himself to receive the cardinalship. He died on June 26, 1988, shortly before

is good), through God's "drama," only to end up discerning and understanding what has been said and done in the form of truth. His trilogy is a multi-volume work, and each aspect of his reflection takes several volumes of its own. The first part is his *Theological Aesthetics* [henceforth, GL1–7]. The second part is the *Theo-Drama* [henceforth abbreviated as TD1–5]. And the last is his *Theo-Logic* [henceforth, abbreviated as TL1–3]. The first work of the *Theo-Logic* was published in 1947 and only later incorporated as the first volume of the *Theo-Logic* in 1985.

48. Balthasar, *Mysterium Paschale*, 176–79. [henceforth MP].

49. He believed it served as a good meditative foundation to show the combined theological ideas he had with Adrienne von Speyr, but he believed the proper theological nuance was not there. Thus, he would further explicate his understanding of Holy Saturday in his Theological Trilogy. See Hofer, "Balthasar's Eschatology on the Intermediate State," 162.

he was to receive that honor. Despite not attaining it, the honor of that appointment stands to show the value the church discerned in Balthasar's service, the value of his theological work, as the then Cardinal Ratzinger (later, Pope Benedict XVI), declared in his homily at Balthasar's funeral service:

> Von Balthasar was hesitant in opening himself for the honor intended for him by his being named to the cardinalate. This was not motivated by a coquettish desire to act the great one, but by the Ignatius spirit which characterized his life. In some way, his being called into the next life on the very eve of being so honored seems to show he was right about it. He was allowed to remain himself, fully. But what the Pope intended to express by this mark of distinction, and of honor, remains valid: no longer only private individuals but the Church itself, in its official responsibility, tells us that he is right in which he teaches of the Faith, that he points the way to the sources of living water—a witness to the word which teaches us Christ and which teaches us how to live.[50]

While Balthasar certainly had critics who questioned his theological enterprise, his supporters, including several Popes, suggested that his work has merit and is worthy of study. He desired to work for and help Christians by giving himself over to Christ, following the theology of obedience he himself presented in his work. At his funeral, the then Cardinal Ratzinger confirmed that he had accomplished his task, indicating to the church, and to critics like Ralph Martin, that whatever problems remain his writings, they are overshadowed by his love for Christ. Unlike Ralph Martin who declared that Balthasar, "departs from the content of revelation and the mainstream theological tradition of the Church,"[51] Ratzinger believed Pope John Paul II had affirmed Balthasar as a faithful teacher of the church's tradition and was worthy of the honor the Pope had wanted to bestow upon him.

50. Ratzinger, "Homily at the Funeral of Hans Urs von Balthasar," 294–95.

51. Martin, *Will Many Be Saved*, 178.

II

The Hope That All Would Be Saved

HOPE ALLOWS FOR PERDITION

PERHAPS WHAT MOST PEOPLE who have not read much from Balthasar have heard about him is his hope that all could be saved. As noted in the introduction, this placed him in a heated debate with theologians who believed he was hiding, through such language, an invalid universalism which must be rejected. Such a theory of universal salvation was not what he was after, as he pointed out in an interview with Angelo Scola:

> I am presently engaged in a confrontation with the German "right," which insists at all costs that one may not hope for the salvation of all men, since there exists full certainty that some will be damned. Such a certainty appears to me unwarranted. For one, the Church has never asserted any man's damnation, and there are numerous New Testament texts pointing in the opposite direction: "God wills all men to be saved," and "If I be lifted up, I will draw all things to myself." There are many such texts. Thus hope for all men seeks to be permitted, as long as one does not seek to anticipate the judgment of the Lord, or preach a theory of universal salvation.[1]

Since he did not know the outcome of the last judgment, Balthasar made it clear he could not know whether or not all will be saved. He believed that he had good reasons to hope all could be saved, but he knew

1. Balthasar, *Test Everything*, 85–86.

his hope had to take into account the possibility of perdition. His hope relied upon the great work of God to reach out to everyone, giving everyone every opportunity to be converted, to have a change of heart, and to be saved. In his theology, perdition can only be had by a complete and utter rejection of the saving work of God. Because there is much confusion as to what Balthasar's hope entailed, it is important to first examine what he meant by it, so that it can be seen why it does not dismiss the possibility of eternal perdition. In doing so, themes will be introduced which will be further elaborated upon later, but they will also be necessary here in order to properly set up what Balthasar's hope did and did not contain.

THE ESCHATOLOGICAL PARADOX WITHIN SCRIPTURE

Balthasar believed Scripture deserved a central place in any proper theology, and so he tried to make sure his theology did not neglect what was contained within it. Such a task was not easy because of how difficult it can be to interpret Scripture properly. Balthasar found this was especially true with the eschatological positions found in Scripture because it could be read as supporting both the possibility of the perdition of some, many or most of humanity as well as the possibility that all might be saved. All that Scripture suggested had to be given equal hearing and acceptance. Many, in reading Scripture, looked at those sayings and statements which warned about perdition and all too quickly believed such texts indicated that some must be among the damned, but they overlooked other passages which suggested that all humanity could end up being saved:

> However, before we draw this apparently inevitable conclusion, we must frankly admit that a great number of passages really do speak in favor of universal salvation; we must give this fact its appropriate place and, as Schleiermacher demands, grant it "at least equal rights" to exist.[2]

Balthasar acknowledged that, as many knew, Scripture warned of the possibility of eternal damnation.[3] What he wanted his readers to recognize is that other verses indicated that Christ's work would be effective for all, so that no one had to be lost. They tell us that Christ's work was intended

2. TD5, 269–70.

3. See, for example, DWH 30–33, where Balthasar listed the following Scriptural verses: Matt 5:25, 8:12, 11:21, 13:42, 13:50, 18:34, 22:37–40, 22:51, 25:30–46; Mark 3:29, 16:16; and Luke 12:10.

to give mercy to all, that is, his work was for the salvation of all.[4] Knowing that some of his readers might simply declare Christ's work to be objective, without having some subjective effect on everyone, Balthasar said that, "The 'all' that recurs again and again in them cannot be limited to a merely 'objective redemption' that would simply leave open the matter of acceptance by particular subjects."[5]

For Balthasar, the difficulty theologians had to face was that there is an eschatological paradox in Scripture. There are verses which apparently contradict each other. Theologians should not toss out a text which said something they found difficult to reconcile with their own theological views; rather, they must adhere to all the teachings contained in Scripture, even when such teachings seem to be in conflict with each other. Only when taken as a whole does Scripture reveal itself.[6] Theologians must be willing to let Scripture's eschatological paradox remain without trying to overcome it by some final systematic solution; they should follow Scripture's direction and let that paradox remain.[7]

In Scripture there is the indication that Christ might save everyone. Christ also warned that some might perish. No one knows which will happen. No one knows what will happen to them until they have gone through

4. See DWH, 33–46 for those verses Balthasar relied upon to demonstrate Christ's universal work, among which are: Col 1:20; Eph 1:10; John 3:16, 16:33; 1 Tim 2:, 2:4–5, 4:10 and Titus 2:11.

5. DWH, 35. This declaration sounds as if there is no possibility of rejecting Christ and that Balthasar really meant Christ saved everyone, which explains why many critics will read him as saying such. But that was not his point. He wanted to affirm that Christ had a subjective engagement with all, and the effect of his work had a real effect one everyone. Death has changed as a result of Christ's death, so now it becomes a trajectory by which all the dead come to meet Christ, where then they shall be judged and find themselves either saved or among the lost.

6. Balthasar, like many readers of Scripture, considered Scripture as a self-interpreting text which must be taken and followed in its final form. Difficult texts are best be understood when looked at and interpreted through the rest of Scripture. Problems emerge when such texts are removed or ignored because of how difficult they are, or if they are taken by themselves and used to dismiss what is revealed in the rest of Scripture. See Dickens, "Balthasar's Biblical Hermeneutics," 181.

7. Clearly Balthasar thought the paradox could be discussed, for he did so. The problem he had was with those who tried to do so without recognizing the limitations placed upon the enterprise. They took their own considerations as final. He understood his position was one of theological hope. He knew the paradox would only be resolved in the eschaton, which is why theological opinions should be open to many different possible endings to history. His conflict was with those who thought they knew the answer before it had been revealed.

Christ's judgment. For it is only in and through that judgment the eschatological ending will be revealed. Until then, it would be in vain to proclaim with certainty anything beyond the judgment to come. Balthasar put it succinctly:

> It is not for man, who is *under* judgment, to construct syntheses here, and above all none of such a kind as to subsume one series of statements under the other, practically emasculating the universalist ones because he believes himself to have 'certain knowledge' of the potency of the first.[8]

Despite his own caveat, Balthasar suggested a way in which he believed Scripture could be read. He stated that those verses which warned of perdition seemed to represent the human situation before Christ's Resurrection from the dead. "As a preliminary we observe that all the Lord's words that refer to the possibility of eternal perdition are pre-Easter words, like John 9:39, where Jesus says that he has come into the world in order to judge it."[9] On the other hand, those offering the hope for the salvation of all come from a post-Easter situation, beginning with Paul's "certainty that, if God is for us, no earthly power can be against us."[10] In this way, Balthasar said that there were two radically different situations discussed in Scripture, each with their own eschatological suggestions. In saying this, Balthasar did not want his readers to believe that verses speaking of the pre-Easter situation had no relevance after Easter. They do, but they must be read and interpreted in the light of the cross. The cross has changed the value of the pre-Easter warnings. They remain in effect but they do so with a new intensity, because the New Testament suggests that there is nothing left by perdition for those who reject the work of Christ on their behalf:

> The enduring gravity of the situation emerges perhaps most clearly in the threats contained in the Letter to the Hebrews, which seems to despair of salvation for those who are not satisfied with the Faith of Christ and fall away from it—however, after the offering up of his Son, God has no other grace to confer (6:4–8; 10:26–31), although a word of consolation and encouragement is always added to these most extreme threats (6:9ff; 10:32ff).[11]

8. DWH, 23.
9. TD5, 279.
10. TD5, 280.
11. DWH, 34.

Easter gave Balthasar the hope that all might be saved. Despite knowing the dangers of doing so, that hope often seems to have taken Balthasar over, so that, from time to time, it can be difficult for the reader to see how he leaves the possibility of perdition intact. It is not that he denied the possibility of perdition but rather he read history in light of his hope. Thus, Geoffrey Wainwright is right when he said, "It seems fair to say that in Balthasar there is a presumption—though without presumptiveness—in favor of God's universal salvific will, which is revealed, or confirmed, by his sending the Son as redeemer."[12] Even though Balthasar favored one side of the eschatological paradox, that "without presumptiveness" is key. Balthasar did not let his hope reject the possibility of perdition nor the need to explain, in some fashion or another, what perdition would entail. Nonetheless, his hope made it difficult for Balthasar to explore the concept of perdition, to explain why the possibility of damnation remained after explaining how everything is changed in the light of Easter, and this certainly explains why critics, engaging a simple reading of his text, end up thinking he is a universalist.

THE CONTEXT OF SIN

Before the accomplishment of Christ, humanity had found itself turned away from God because of sin. Salvation is the reorientation of humanity so that it is once again turned towards God. Sin deserves condemnation but God's love for humanity sent Jesus into the world so that sinners could be reconciled with God and not perish due to God's judgment of sin:

> All of us were sinners before him and worthy of condemnation. But God 'made the One who knew no sin to be sin, so that we might be justified through him in God's eyes' (2 Cor 5:21). Only God in his absolute freedom can take hold of our finite freedom from within in such a way as to give it a direction toward him, an exit to him, when it was closed in on itself.[13]

No matter how they described it, Balthasar believed that impact of sin upon humanity was something universally acknowledged by world religions. They tried to find a way to understand justice in a world in which the presence of evil could be felt and the solution was through some sort of

12. Wainwright, "Eschatology," 122.

13. Balthasar, *A Short Primer For Unsettled Laymen*, 86.

judgment of that evil. "The presence of injustice and of personal social guilt in the world is too pressing for all of the religions of the world not to have tried to work for a solution to untangle the snarl; and this has always been with the idea of some kind of judgment."[14]

Christianity shows the nature of sin, how it darkens the human condition, turning everyone away from the truth. "Sin is essentially untruth, a lie that seeks to release from itself, once it has become personal and social, a pseuduoform of secondary 'truth' as the normal form, which is taken as valid as a mere matter of course."[15] Sin establishes in its wake a falsehood pretending to be truth which clouds the mind, making it see and believe things to be true which are not.[16] It makes everyone suffer as they know death comes, a death that somehow connects with the evil which exists in the world. Sin makes everyone suffer, and indeed, it not only is caused by sinners, but as they suffer from their sin, it makes sinners turn further away from God, making for an impossible situation for sinners. "The anxiety of the wicked is both effect and cause of their turning away from God; it encloses and incarcerates; it is the sign of God's wrath set up over them. . ."[17]

Those who are trapped by sin cannot claim anything about the outcome of their eschatological judgment, for they live under the domain of sin and its contamination on the mind. Despite feeling its dread effects upon their lives, they continue to sin. Even Christians, insofar as they live in themselves, turned in upon themselves and not towards God, experience this anxiety. "To place oneself on this solid ground involves relinquishing one's own ground. The sinner wants to stand on his own, not on God. And whoever tries to stand both on God and on his own is sure to fall into the bottomless space in between."[18] It is unbelief, a lack of faith or trust in God, which turns Christians away from God and back to the anxiety of the wicked.[19] This must not be interpreted to suggest that as long as a Christian has faith in God, they know the outcome of their own eschatological judgment and that they will be saved. Rather, they have hope, not presumption, and

14. Balthasar, *Explorations in Theology IV*, 444. [Henceforth ET4].

15. ET4, 444.

16. See Balthasar, *The Christian and Anxiety*, 48–49.

17. Ibid., 67.

18. Ibid., 99–100.

19. See ibid., 101.

they must allow God to act and decide the eschaton for them instead of giving him their eschatological demands.[20]

GOD'S LOVE LIES BEHIND GOD'S ACTIONS TOWARD SIN

Balthasar believed that sin had to be taken seriously. God took sin seriously. God warned humanity of what happens when any of them should sin. Because of sin, God is angered. Scripture reveals many warnings given out by God with the threat of eternal perdition for those who remain in sin. It reveals God's wrath. Even in the New Testament, God's wrath over sin is manifest:

> Paul is thoroughly acquainted with talk of the wrath of God. The last judgment is as terrifying for him (Rom 2:5: "By your unrepentant heart you pile up for yourself wrath at the day of wrath") as it was for the people of the Old Covenant, for the Baptist, for Jesus himself (see Lk 21:23). Yet even now "God's wrath from heaven above reveals itself' without restraint 'against all godlessness and unrighteousness of men, who suppress the truth in their wickedness" (Rom 1:18).[21]

God's wrath cannot be seen apart from his holiness and love. Balthasar believed that they were interconnected.[22] It is love which leads to God's anger. "The love in God's heart is laid bare in all its radicality, showing its absolute opposition to anything that would injure it."[23] Sin is justly condemned by God, but God's condemnation always works with his mercy, indeed, his wrath over sin acts as a function of his mercy:

> So in no way does it exclude his mercy; in fact, it should be regarded as a function of mercy, as we find in certain daring expressions of the divine mercy: 'In overflowing wrath for a moment I hid my face from you, but with everlasting love I will have compassion on you' (Is 54:8); 'For his anger is but for a moment, and his favor is for a lifetime' (Ps 30:5).[24]

20. See ibid., 146–48.

21. Balthasar, *You Have Words of Eternal Life*, 62–63.

22. See Vasko, "Suffering and the Search for Wholeness," 115.

23. TD4, 341.

24. TD4, 340.

The connection between God's wrathful judgment with God's mercy and love is revealed in its fullness in the cross. Nonetheless, it can also be understood in the way God's wrath, revealed in his moral law and the words of the prophets, worked for the correction of sinners. The warnings of perdition, found throughout Scripture, come out of God's love, revealing the possibility of doom but also giving room for sinners to respond to God's notification and to become the people he wanted them to be. An example of this can be found in the story of Jonah. The mission God gave to Jonah was to warn Nineveh of their impending doom. The warning was true, Nineveh had been judged by God, condemned for its evil. Jonah revealed God's anger over Nineveh's sins. Yet, the people of Nineveh heard Jonah, repented, and did not perish. Jonah was disturbed by this, for he believed his words were not conditional, but necessary. He did not entirely understand, as many others do not understand, the point of God's warnings. They are given to correct sinners. They state what will happen without such correction, not whether or not sinners will repent. This is why, when looking at Scripture and its message about hell, the question is not whether or not the condemnation is correct, but whether or not those who hear the warning will repent, or if they will not turn from their sins and so be condemned. So many see the threat of hell in Scripture and believe it means they know some will go there. "Is the transition from threat to the *knowledge* that it will be carried out necessary?"[25] The answer, shown by the example of Jonah, is no. God's love seeks after the salvation of all, even if his wrath shows his just judgment over sin.

HOPE FROM LOVE

For Balthasar, the possibility of perdition was real, but the hope that people will turn from their sins and be saved was also real. Scripture showed him how God's pronouncements concerning sin must not be read outside of the context of God's love. Because of his great love for humanity, God desires that all be saved, and speaks in such a way to correct sinners so that they can turn from their sins. It gives God a "hope" that all shall be saved through the work he does for us. It was this love which fostered Balthasar's own hope that all might be saved. Those who love God will follow God in hoping for the salvation of all, doing what they can to bring it into effect:

25. DWH, 183. It should be noted that in the original German, *Drohung* (threat) and not *Wissen* (knowledge) is in italics.

> Just as God so loved the world that he completely handed over his Son for its sake, so too the one whom God has loved will want to save himself only in conjunction with those who have been created with him, and he will not reject the share of penitential suffering that he has been given for the sake of the whole. He will do so in Christian hope, the hope for the salvation of all men, which is permitted to Christians alone.[26]

Love is fundamental to Balthasar's theology of salvation and perdition. Love cannot be separated from God's justice. Love gives hope that all might be saved, and seeks after that possibility, while it is also love which lies behind the dark, dire warnings of perdition. God seeks love from all. He is angered by our sin, for sin shows we do not properly return God's love for us with love for him. God's anger is therefore a manifestation of his love. Yet, because his anger is only understood as an aspect of his love, love is the hermeneutic which prevails, which is why love can prevail over the just demands of God's anger:

> The seriousness that we are confronted with is the seriousness of a love that goes beyond all justice. God's love for every man is absolute; it is ineffable. Who can, "by rights," claim adequacy before it? No saint would presume to say "I can." No one has loved God with his whole heart, with his whole soul, with all his strength. Everyone, without exception, has to say: "Lord, I am not worthy."[27]

While no one is worthy of his love, God looks for anything which represents engagement with him and his grace, anything which represents a loving response back to him, so that he can use it to redeem the sinner and bring about their salvation. This is manifest at the last judgment, where such love is the means by which God will make his ruling:

> Here the Judge will ascertain "whether there is something in the life of the one to be judged that fits into this relationship of love, that *has* been taken up into his living love, or *can* be taken up, or at least could be as a possibility of faith, something at all that is capable of love," a "little seed of love" in response to all the love bestowed upon him by God."[God] "wishes to give him the possibility of receiving at least a part of his grace within the framework created by his refusal."[28]

26. LA, 97.

27. DWH, 176.

28. TD5, 296, quoting Adrienne von Speyr's commentaries on 1 John and 2 John,

All that God needs to find to in a sinner is a little remnant of love, and it will provide him the means by which the sinner could be saved.

HOPE IS NOT CERTAINTY

God loves the world and seeks the salvation of all. Balthasar made it clear that God will do all that he could to accomplish this goal. He will look for any and all manifestations of love to work with and bring about the salvation of a sinner. However, he will do so in the manner which does not remove free will from his creatures.[29] They have been given freedom, and God does not override it as if turning them into puppets. "Human freedom, which lives and operates entirely within the inspiration pouring forth from the God, who is always eternally free, is not in any way a puppet play, the deterministic result of string-pulling; this is evident from the Christology that speaks of two wills in the incarnate Son."[30] God will do what he can to persuade his creatures to turn themselves away from their sins and to turn toward him, but he will not make that decision for them.

With all that God can do to persuade sinners, it is often asked, will someone hold out and deny God? It is hard to believe that if God were doing everything he could to convert sinners to himself that he would be denied. Indeed, some of what Balthasar wrote makes it difficult to understand why anyone would, in the end, deny God.[31] Yet the answer is yes, it must remain possible. Those who refuse now might turn to God later, but will everyone do so? Or will there be someone who perpetually denies God to the very end? There is no answer which can be given to this question this side of the eschaton.[32] Even if such a rejection would end up being inexplicable, that it

revealing how he will use her own words and mix them with his to make for a unified theological statement from the two of them. He wanted to force the reader to accept von Speyr's authority if they are going to accept his own pronouncements. She provided the experience necessary for theological explorations, making it more than a mere rationalistic enterprise.

29. As Margaret Turek explained, Balthasar did not want to pit God's freedom over human freedom as if God's greatness ended up overpowering human freedom, rendering it as nothing. Instead, the goal was to find a way to show how God's love, freely given to his creation, left room for his creation to respond to him with their own love. See Turek, "'As the Father loved me' (Jn 15:9): Towards a Theology of God the Father," 272.

30. TD5, 410.

31. See Pitstick, *Light in Darkness*, 272.

32. "The question to which no final answer is given, or can be given is this: Will he who refuses it now refuse it to the last?" DWH, 178.

seems foolish that anyone should deny God's grace once they understood what it could do for them, for human freedom to be recognized, the freedom to deny God had to remain a possibility.

THE MYSTERY OF SIN

Balthasar made it clear that on this side of the eschaton no one could know how people have responded to God's love, whether or not they have fully rejected it through sin or responded to it with love of their own and so received God's saving grace into their lives. How they responded to God will be made known to them and to everyone else after their death, after they have ended their activity in the drama of world history. Yet, the disclosure of their eschatological character will be based upon how they responded to God and his offer of grace throughout their lives, so that it truly is what they have done with their lives which determines the outcome of their lives. History is real, and its implications are real, but what those implications are will only be revealed in the eschaton.

Why, if everyone is offered the opportunity for salvation, would some end up rejecting it? Behind this question lies the mystery of sin. It is sin that leads people away from God, and it is through attachment to sin, some might end up lost. What is sin? Why do people sin? Why does God even allow sin? What culpability does someone have for their sin if it come from situations outside of their control, where they sin either out of ignorance, or they are forced to act against their will so that some external force makes them sin?

For Balthasar, sin is irrational and so defies explanation. Any attempt to explain sin undermines this irrationality, because explanations are founded upon reason while sin itself has no rationale to hold it together. This is not to say theology cannot discuss sin, cannot get some insight into sin, but in doing so, the mystery of sin lies behind all explanations and so renders all such explanations unsatisfactory.

Yet, Balthasar believed that the mystery must be acknowledged and even explored. Contrary to his friend Karl Barth, he thought it was necessary to consider why someone would sin, and to do that was to recognize sin was itself the negative response of a person to God's overture of love toward them. If grace and salvation are found in love, sin and perdition are found in the rejection of that love, that is, in hate. The more God shows forth love to someone, the more those stuck in sin will respond with increasing hate.

For sin to lead to perdition, it must be as endless as God's love is infinite, as Balthasar explained: "Here, once again, we come up against the *Mysterium iniquitatis*, and it is impossible simply to avert our eyes from it as Karl Barth suggests we should. This is central to the mystery of the theodrama: God's heightened love provokes a heightened hatred that is as bottomless as love itself (Jn 15:25)."[33]

Sin connects to human freedom by corrupting it, changing its modality, so that the original mode of freedom, the freedom of love, is changed to what is known as an indifferent freedom of choice, the kind of choice people generally consider to be what freedom is about because it is the kind of freedom to which they have become accustomed. Before sin manifested itself in humanity through the sin of Adam, it had to exist in potentiality. Why did God allow for this potential, and why exactly, did Adam turn it into reality? To read the question through the lens of indifferent freedom is to misunderstand the original form of freedom given to humanity, and so not to understand what original sin was and how it deformed the human character. It was not an indifferent choice between good and evil:

> To begin with the *liberum arbitrium* as one's point of departure is to presuppose something that cannot be legitimately presupposed with certainty: the knowledge of good and evil, or, what amounts to the same thing, the pernicious neutrality and indifference toward good and evil, with respect to God and anti-God. God did not set his creature in this bad position; indeed, the whole point of the prohibition in paradise was to preserve his creature from it.[34]

The initial state was free, not in the arbitrary sense of freedom of indifference, but the freedom of a lover to follow the beloved or to deny them. "The beloved good that is totally present to the lover relieves him of all choice: he is the one who is decided, who has no other choice, and who experiences therein his entire freedom and liberation."[35] In this way, Balthasar suggested that love has its own modality of freedom which humanity followed before it sinned. Love chooses the beloved naturally, while sin interferes with that love, and makes the choice based upon other determinations than the natural tendency to love the beloved. When freedom is engaged through love, its outcome is not an issue of indeterminate choice:

33. TD5, 285.

34. Balthasar, *Christian and Anxiety*, 134.

35. Ibid., 135.

> To one who loves, it would seem the rankest disloyalty to set beside the beloved a second possible object of choice in order, by a kind of qualitative analysis, to give the preference to the first. Such indifference about the object of its choice may be an initial stage on the road to love; but within love itself it has no place. Love is so steadfast that it never reverts to the point of indifference that precedes choice. It rejects "freedom of choice" in favor of freedom of love.[36]

The mode of freedom found in the freedom to love is lost and turned to indifferent freedom when love is weakened or lost. The origin of indifferent freedom as the modality of human freedom can be found in the fall of Adam, when Adam withdrew from his love for God. He had not yet truly seen God face to face, that is, he has not been given the beatific vision; he knew God and walked with God, but was still given the chance to determine for himself his character, that is, if he would follow after God in love or if he would follow something else with his love instead. Adam knew God, but God kept himself at a distance from Adam so that Adam's love could be tested. If he had chosen to follow God with that love, he would have been welcomed to the beatific vision, but since he loved something other than God over God, Adam lost an element of God's presence in his life, creating a void within which then became the foundation for his new modality of willing, a void which he shares with the rest of his progeny, that is, the whole of humanity:

> We are only saying here that the space within Adam that became a place of emptiness and indifferent freedom through the withdrawal of the divine presence was a space that God had originally created for himself and had filled with his mysterious, and, on the other hand, unquestionable presence.[37]

When love no longer guides the will, then the modality of freedom changes, so that choices are made not through the guidance of love, but in and through the darkened intellect which has to make choices based upon its imperfect understanding of the choices which lie before it. Sin is often the result of such ignorance, because the sinner will act in accordance to a misperception of the good, following an imperfect good away from the fullness of the good found in and with God. Likewise, the sinner will not be able to love properly because all things will be seen in the light of such

36. Balthasar, *The Christian State of Life*, 30.

37. Balthasar, *Christian and Anxiety*, 135.

partiality, objectifying the world in that partiality, so that love will be had for an object and not the subject behind the object, making even the act of love the enemy of love itself.[38]

How, then, did Adam sin? Balthasar understood that whatever answer given to this question, there will remain an element of ambiguity.[39] There had to be a way for Adam to be created good in a loving relationship with God, and yet he had to have the freedom given to him that he could turn away from God, turn away from love, and so embrace sin. Key to Balthasar's answer lies in the fact that Adam was established in a state which was meant to be the foundation, but not the end, of his encounter with God. He was meant to open himself up to God with love, so that God could then grant him deifying beatitude. Adam's original state, while good, was not the final state God intended for him.[40] This meant there was even in his creation a space which God gave to Adam in which God allowed Adam to determine how it would be filled, whether or not he would open it up to God to be filled by the grace of God, or if he would close it off from God and attach it to something else, expanding that space and creating a void within, the void of sin. This space was necessary if Adam were to be free, and in his freedom, free to love God or not. This space was the place in which Adam could be tempted: "But God had to leave open to man the space that made it possible for man to move away from God. And God could not spare man the experience of being tempted by what God had excluded and forbidden, which precisely by being forbidden acquires its power over man."[41] Through Adam, the space became the void of sin, and this void became a part of the human psyche, a space which God was meant to occupy was instead occupied by nothingness. Humanity feels this lack of the presence of God, causing them great angst, for, "what makes anxiety anxious is the awareness of a fundamental falsehood, displacement, guilt—an awareness called forth by the absence of the One who ought to be present in this 'Nothing.'"[42]

38. In this manner, David Crawford suggested that indifferent freedom establishes itself as the enemy of true love, and if it is an enemy of true love, then it is an enemy of true freedom found in love. See Crawford, "Love, Action, and Vows," 305.

39. See Balthasar, *Christian and Anxiety*, 136.

40. See ibid., 140.

41. Ibid., 141.

42. Ibid., 142.

Balthasar's description of the fall shows once again any discussion of sin reveals sin is going to be a mystery. How sin is explained will counter what sin is, for sin cannot be explained. Even the way the choice made by Adam is explained by Balthasar finds itself resembling more the indifferent freedom which is supposed to come after the fall than it does with the freedom of love which is said to be the modality of freedom before sin contaminated the human psyche. Why would someone not choose God if they are given that option and they truly knew what that option was and their choice was motivated not by ignorance but by love? Again, it ties with the mystery of sin. Sin somehow short circuited that love. The choice not to love God must have been based upon the choice to love something other than God, closing off God's presence from the space made for him in the human person.

Now, the mystery of sin continues, but it is a mystery which contains within it the indifferent freedom which makes it easier to explain. Those who do not choose God do so because they think they will find greater happiness apart from God. What they do, directly or indirectly, is choose themselves as the center of their being. This does not give them what they would expect. They seek themselves as the source of their happiness but they cannot give it to themselves. It is easy to understand why someone might, out of ignorance, choose themselves over God. Such ignorance is not permanent. Balthasar believed that the Holy Spirit will illuminate everyone with grace and show them the outcome of such a hold to the self and where it leads. Why, when that happens, some would remain obstinate and still reject God is the real mystery. But it is clear to Balthasar that it is necessary for God to give everyone every chance to be reconciled with him. Perdition is not something that comes to a person unaware, as if they had no chance of salvation, but rather, it can only come after a knowing rejection of God's grace. The Holy Spirit works to bring that knowledge to everyone, so that it is only in the Holy Spirit people can truly we turn away from God and become attached to themselves:

> Tentatively, we can say this: that the Holy Spirit, the Spirit of absolute freedom, allows us to see, within our free spirit, what our *own* true freedom would be, that is, by confronting us with ourself, with our highest possibility. We *would* not *be able* just to say "Yes" to ourselves (that is effected for us vicariously); also, the meaningfulness of such a "Yes" and the *desire for it* are set before us,

> indeed, inspired in us. Do you really want to exist forevermore in contradiction with yourself?[43]

Whether or not this revelation of the Spirit will lead someone to turn themselves over entirely to God and away from their grasping of themselves as the center of being will determine what kind of grace is associated with this revelation: it is said to be efficient grace if it leads someone to truly turn toward God, and it is sufficient grace if it does not.[44] What is important here is that God works with all, providing the grace, the revelation, needed for their conversion, and such opportunities may or may not be met with *metanoia*. Sinners, when shown what God offers them, might turn toward God and give God the love which is his due, or they still can refuse God when confronted by what God offers them, but they will do so knowingly and without question. This confrontation comes from God's loving grace, and any obstinate "no" to that grace remains mysterious, for it makes no sense as to why someone would willingly decline the happiness which would occur if they allow God to make them perfect. Nonetheless, the possibility of such a rejection remains, and Balthasar made sure it was not dismissed.

Is there not something about Balthasar's presentation which makes it difficult to believe anyone would really choose against their own good and deny God? Yes, sin is a mystery and the rejection of God, as sin, might not be comprehensible. Who would ever deny God if they truly understood the happiness that God offers them? Balthasar, it seems, was stacking the deck in favor of hope. Was it intentional, or was it because sin is incomprehensible and so any attempt to explain it will fail and will appear to be stacking the deck against sin? It would seem the latter is most likely. His focus was on the hope that all could be saved; he grasped it better, and so all discussions, even those which touched on the question of perdition, were filtered in the light of that hope. Yet he did not deny the possibility that some could be lost; he had a difficulty explaining it in light of his understanding of what

43. DWH, 209.

44. DWH, 209. Balthasar's explanation here for sufficient grace is that it is when a subject seeing the possible perfection offered "cannot do other than *freely* seize itself." How can a subject freely act in a way that it cannot act but the way it acts and still be called free? The answer for Balthasar lies in his understanding of the higher, original mode of freedom, that of the modality of love: love dictates the decision. Everyone is free to act in accordance to where they have placed their love. If their love has become entirely closed to God, then it will lead them to turn away from God even when offered his love.

God does for everyone to help make sure they are saved, but the difficulty lies in the fact that sin is irrational and acts contrary to the dictates of logic. Logic will suggest everyone should seek after what is best for themselves, but sin encourages them to do the opposite. Any explanation will itself touch upon some element of logic which exists apart from the irrationality of sin, so any explanation will fail to account why anyone truly would will to sin. This is why Balthasar will explore in detail the conditions for perdition, so that tragedy is a possible end for the divine drama, but he will not do so in a way which definitively explains why any particular person would be lost. It is an issue of freedom, a freedom which is preserved in the eschaton, which serves as the foundation for is agnostic answer as to the fate of humanity in the eschaton itself.

AUGUSTINE AND THE *MASSA DAMNATA*

The central concern of Balthasar's eschatology is that no one must presume to know what God has not revealed. Except for the saints, no one knows the eschatological fate of those who have already died, even as no one knows the fate of those living in the world today.[45] Scripture both warns that some could be lost, but it also offers the hope for salvation. It is paramount that no one presumes themselves to be among the saved, even as they must not presume for others that they are among the damned, because such presumption transcends what God has revealed.[46] Yet, as history shows, im-

45. The declaration that some are saved and are among the saints of God is not presumption because God has shown the world their eschatological fate as a witness to the beatitude we can all experience. They have died, and in their death they have passed over to the eschaton themselves. The veneration of the saints is not presumption but the celebration that they realized God's charism for them, that God has revealed to the church that they are indeed among the saved, and so they are worthy of being celebrated and honored by the church: "The person who has become dispossessed by his mission becomes a universal, anonymous principle of fruitfulness. This anonymity is at the root of the 'communion of saints.' Anyone who allows himself to be dispossessed by God and his mission is a foundation stone of community, a place whence others can draw sustenance and find materials with which to build themselves up. Essentially, every saint is holy, not for himself but for God and his fellow men." Balthasar, *You Crown the Year With Your Goodness*, 206–7.

46. Edward Oakes in *Patterns of Redemption* summarizes both Balthasar's hope and angst well: "The point is, there *is* a wrath to come, but because of the solidarity of the human race in Adam, it is directed at all of us; and because Christ reversed the curse of Adam on the Cross and thereby saved all men (Rm 5:15), God's grace of redemption is directed at all (Rm 11:32). What, then, of individual fate? Will not God, 'give to each

portant theologians and saints have presumed that many will be damned. Does this not bring into question whether or not he was right in hoping that all could be saved?[47]

Balthasar believed that Augustine, and the Augustinian tradition, was central in the development of the notion that more people will be damned than not. Augustine popularized the view, and, because Augustine was the recognized theological authority of the West, the possibility of a mass number of the damned was often seen as more than a mere possibility, but as a fact.[48]

This meant Balthasar had to offer many criticisms of Augustine's theology. Yet, despite such criticisms, Balthasar did not want to dismiss Augustine's theological contributions. He wanted to contextualize them and find the good in Augustine's ideas through such contextualization. Balthasar found much value in Augustine's theology. He especially liked the aesthetic appeal of Augustine's theology, the kind of appeal Balthasar believed was needed for proper theological work. Thus, when dealing with Augustine, Balthasar did not want to dismiss the aesthetic which led to Augustine's ideas. In Augustine, God works with sin and finds a place for it, putting it in its proper place in the cosmos, allowing it to form a part of an aesthetically appealing whole. For Augustine, the proper place for sinners is hell, and the damned have a place in the cosmos because they can be used as a contrast to the glorious beauty of the saved. Augustine suggested that there needed to be a variety of beings, leading to a variety of levels of holiness in creation; ugliness and evil was needed to show that which is beautiful and good to be truly beautiful and good.[49] Balthasar, of course, did not want to suggest that Augustine believed God made people sin, for obviously, God does not want sin. However, once sin entered the world, God had to deal with it, and Augustine believed that way was how God dealt with them aestheti-

---

person according to what he has done' (Rm 2:6)? Yes, definitely! But who can anticipate *for others* how the judgment will turn out—especially if even St. Paul (!) cannot anticipate his own fate before God's throne?" Oakes, *Pattern of Redemption*, 309.

47. Critics of Balthasar often question whether or not Balthasar is doing justice to the theological tradition by ignoring or outright rejecting what so many in tradition has said. To such critics Balthasar could reply that the opinion of everyone within the tradition, and not just some of them, is what is important.

48. See DWH, 164–65.

49. Balthasar believed this became a common feature of eschatological aesthetics found after Augustine, such as found in the eschatologies of scholastic writers like St. Bonaventure. See GL2, 331.

cally, finding the proper place for them in hell. Balthasar considered this reasoning to be inspired, at least in part, from Augustine's pre-Christian background.[50] His Manichean education left Augustine with tendencies he would have to wrestle with and against throughout his theological career. Augustine would have to find a way to differentiate himself from his former religious affiliation. When Augustine explained the place of sin and hell in creation, Balthasar believed the difference with the Catholic Augustine with the Manichaean Augustine was the details Augustine developed to explain his system, and yet, underneath those details, Augustine was quick to accept notions from his former adherence which theologians continue to wrestle with to this day:

> However, God is powerful enough to find a place for immanent disorder in his transcendent order and to fit it into the higher harmony. Augustine has to press his arguments against the Manichees into the finest points of detail, and, tentatively but firmly, he makes no exception for the suffering of the irrational creation, not even for the sufferings of innocent children, for suicide nor finally for the existence of hell.[51]

Balthasar believed Augustine's thoughts were readily accepted into the Christian tradition without sufficient critical examination and purification of unseemly theological views. It was not that Augustine's ideas did not lead him beyond the Manichaean tradition, but rather, the remnants of that tradition could be found in his writings, and often readily accepted when they should have been examined and excised by his followers. Augustine's successors gave his secondary opinions and speculations more value than they deserved.

Balthasar's views about Augustine were not meant to undermine Augustine's legitimate place in the history of Christian doctrine, but rather, to remind Christians that any particular writer, no matter how important their contribution to Christian theology, could still make mistakes, and those mistakes must be found and worked out by future generations. Thus, Augustine was a great figure of faith and theology for Balthasar, and many of Augustine's themes were accepted by Balthasar and used to establish his own eschatological views. Augustine's views on love, for example, were taken up by Balthasar.[52] Indeed, Balthasar believed Augustine's discussions

50. DWH, 165.

51. GL2, 127–28.

52. Another Augustinian notion which Balthasar found important was Augustine's

about love could be seen as the beginning of something different and new, and if developed further, Balthasar believed that they offered a different way to engage eschatological questions than Augustine had proposed; it is in this fashion Balthasar acknowledged such an Augustinian influence in his own theology.[53] Balthasar's notion on freedom as a product of love is clearly Augustinian in influence.[54] Proper freedom concerns the will, and love is an act of the will:

> Freedom contains the possibility of preferring, of choice (and the reverse), but freedom itself is free only in the measure that it rightly *(recte)* prefers the right and justly *(juste)* prefers the just. It is sovereign in the measure that it conducts itself by the rule of the absolute: such conduct contains all virtue, and fulfilling happiness (*vita beata*) supervenes both as its immanent result and as the freely given reward (*praemium*). Only if a man sets a direct course to God is every possibility of error eliminated, and the concept of 'happiness', like the 'concept of truth' imprinted (*impressa*) a priori on both rational and moral striving (the two are one), not as an 'innate idea', but as identical with striving itself.[55]

MASSA DAMNATA AND PIOUS TRADITION

While playing a central role in the notion of a *massa damnata,* Augustine was not the only one who proclaimed this teaching. Throughout pious tradition, writings and sayings of many saints and mystics seemed to complement Augustine's thesis. There can be found in the writings and lives of the saints the suggestion that some of them had witnessed hell, and they had confirmed through their experience of hell the *massa damnata*. Balthasar believed this tradition was important, and could not be denied, but he believed that their experiences were misunderstood, sometimes by the saints themselves. There was no way their experience could have been of the eschatological fate of humanity, because they had not yet gone through the eschatological judgment themselves. What they experienced should only

focus on Christ as the center of being, the foundation by which creation will be able to demonstrate the truth and goodness of God. See Daley, "Balthasar's Reading of the Church Fathers," 199.

53. See Nichols, *The Word Has Been Abroad,* 78–79.

54. GL2, 136.

55. GL2, 113.

be seen as a warning about the possibility of hell, encouraging them to follow through with a holy life. If it were truly the experience of perdition, it would offer them no hope, and yet that is what happened. "The hell that is brought before their eyes does not at all produce resignation in them but fires their resolve to resist it more strongly than ever."[56] Or, if they were already holy, it gave them a greater grace, where they shared in the experience of Christ's descent into hell.[57] This view, he believed, was supported, by Adrienne von Speyr, who also had the experience of hell, but for her, it was clearly a sharing in with the passion of Christ, experiencing the horror and shame that Christ felt in the experience of death as it existed apart from the resurrection of the dead.[58] In either case, they did not see past the last judgment, and so what they witnessed could not be the fate of humanity after the last judgment.

Balthasar did not discount that in their experience of hell, the saints saw the images and likenesses of sinners in hell, but these images revealed only what was a possible outcome for sin. As the eschaton could not be experienced, what was seen by the saints represented the possible end of a sinner apart from the resurrection and glorification of Christ. That is, the saints saw what sin is capable of producing in any sinner who does not rise up with Christ and overcome their sin. They saw sinners before their full integration into Christ. Balthasar believed Dante's *Divine Comedy* is representative of this tradition, wherein Dante's hell shows the misery and defeat of sinners in the abode of the dead as they are in themselves apart from Christ's victory over death and sin. Only in purgatory and heaven does the tragedy become a comedy and the grace of Christ penetrate and reveal the possibility of salvation.[59]

The experience of the saints showed them what hell could be like, and gave them material which they could use to warn sinners that they could end up among the lost. Balthasar suggested their claims should be taken similar to the contemplations of hell in the *Spiritual Exercises* of St. Ignatius of Loyola. Balthasar, it could be said, used his Jesuit training with Ignatian Retreats as the hermeneutical lens to explain the experiences of

56. DWH, 216.

57. See DWH, 217.

58. See Speyr, *Book of All Saints*, 14–15.

59. While there is some acknowledgement of the work of Christ beginning to be manifest in the *Inferno*, Balthasar believed that Dante did not distinguish the realm of the dead as it existed before Christ and after, which is why there is a confusion as to what is revealed in Dante's hell. See GL3, 100–1.

hell by found in pious tradition.[60] In this way, he found the foundation for his interpretive scheme.

Nonetheless, Balthasar thought there was something more to be said about the experiences of the saints. They often experienced the sufferings of hell for themselves. Such an experience was purgative for them, and it is through such experiences, they became the holy saints the church recognized them to be. For this notion, Balthasar turned to the thought of St. John of the Cross.[61] "The challenge of St. John of the Cross is that he flings the old slogan, 'God alone suffices', in the face of a world increasingly convinced of its own importance, and he does this with an exclusiveness that effectively makes the realization of 'man in truth' the preserve of a few."[62] Sinners must be transformed from within, transcend everything in the world and see that there is nothing in it, nada, which is of permanent value, so that they can experience the world as it is, allowing for and recognizing the relative good contained within it without absolutizing that good.[63] The purging which comes to us is not like the experience of Dante; the sinner sees the loneliness of hell, where they make their very selves the condition for their hell. "But it is a demythologized night; there is no Virgil for a guide, no conversations with the damned; I myself am Hell."[64] In this purification, sinners are cut off from everything and experience sheer alienation. The soul being purged will experience the pain of hell; but because it is grace which comes to them, the pains are not the end, instead, they form the foundation by which sin can be removed. God lets the soul really come to know itself and feel itself apart from God so that it reacts with an openness to God, ready to turn to God and away from its sinful tendencies which isolate it from God by encouraging the soul to turning in upon itself. The soul experiences such isolation as hell, but in reality it has been placed in

60. See DWH, 217. St. Ignatius's fifth exercise of the first week is a meditation on hell, where one is called "to see with the eyes of the imagination the length, breadth and depth of hell," St. Ignatius of Loyola, *Saint Ignatius of Loyola*, 298. For the saints, God's grace helped supply what was lacking with their imagination so that they could truly see and experience the depths of hell.

61. See GL3, 109–12.

62. GL3, 109.

63. This is manifest in the poetry of St. John of the Cross. As Louis Dupré pointed out, what St. John first rejects through the path of purification emerges once again in his own poetic endeavors; for St. John of the Cross appears to decry images, to be an iconoclast, but his poetry brings them out in their relativized form, able to be used to point beyond themselves to the state beyond images. See Dupré, "The Glory of the Lord," 195.

64. GL3, 110.

purgatory. "Abandonment is experienced subjectively as the fire of Hell, but from God's perspective it is the fire of Purgatory."[65]

Thus, what Balthasar concluded about the experience of hell by mystics is that their experiences must not be interpreted eschatologically, as if they experienced what was to happen after the last judgment of Christ, but rather as something along the path to the eschaton. They give us a warning of the real possibility of perdition and a representation of the kind of purification all must undergo before beatitude. To use pious legends as proof of a *massa damnata* was to misunderstand what the experiences of the saints were meant to teach us, reifying the purgatorial fire as the final fire of perdition.

HOPE IS NOT *APOKATASTASIS*

Balthasar knew how many of his critics suggested that he believed in universal salvation, that he was teaching some sort of *apokatastasis*. He agreed with them that such a doctrine could not be held, but he believed it was for the same reason why a teaching of the necessary damnation of anyone could not be taught. We do not know what lies beyond the last judgment. The problem with the teaching of *apokatastasis* is that it claims to have such knowledge, and so eliminates creaturely freedom. However, that is also the problem which emerges from those who demand a large portion of humanity as being damned. It goes beyond what we can know, and through claims of such knowledge, it ends up removing the value of human freedom. Freedom is important for Balthasar. To give humanity freedom means God must risk losing some, many, or even all of them, but it also gives God greater return for his love if they come back to him with love. God risks that outcome because of his love for his creation.[66]

65. GL3, 111.

66. In GL3, 498–501, Balthasar's exploration of the theological significance of the thought of Charles Péguy contains an elaborate and important demonstration of what this risk entails. Péguy's writings demonstrate why God must make that risk, because they show it is the heart of God behind that risk. Jesus, the Good Shepherd, goes looking for the lost sheep, the sinner, but whether or not he will find them lies with the sinner, whether or not the sinner will return to him. To create and give freedom to creation is in the heart of God, creating therefore a risk for that freedom to go against God's hope for creation. Yet such freedom is sustained by God because he loves his creation. It prevents the creation of some Hegelian synthesis which tries to determine the fate of creation, because such synthesis is founded upon imposing necessity over freedom which God does not do. Apokatastasis can be said to be such a synthesis and so must be rejected.

Balthasar saw that it was easy to confuse the erroneous view of *apokatastasis* with the hope that all might be saved. Some who seemed to teach *apokatastasis*, Balthasar believed, were more cautious than their critics often gave them credit. Origen served as a prime example of this. Balthasar suggested that Origen was more speculative and circumspect than later readers of Origen would allow him to be.[67] Indeed, Origen, when asked, denied that Satan would be saved.[68] Yet Origen read eschatology within a Platonic hermeneutic given to him from the time and place he lived; this is why in his speculative thought, Origen conceived of a cyclical notion of time, a notion which suggested to him that all things will return to their original state in the eschaton, and so, in a sense, all things would be saved.[69]

In contemporary theological circles, many have once again taken up the possibility of *apokatastasis*, in part as a reaction to concerns coming from Augustine's eschatology. This was how Balthasar would understand the eschatology of Karl Barth. Balthasar suggested that Barth freed himself from Augustine by reaching back beyond Augustine to the Alexandrian tradition, and with it, Barth was able to come to establish an alternative eschatology which promoted a sense of *apokatastasis*.[70] Barth did so, however, with modern tools. Dialectic gave to Barth the means by which he would look at the relationship between God and the world, and so through dialectic, once the non-existence of evil was put into the equation, systematic conclusions could be made which would suggest the necessary conclusion that all would be saved.[71]

Balthasar believed that grace must be something which can be resisted. Barth, however, looked as the Lordship of Christ made this resistance futile. In this way, Balthasar claimed that Barth had an absolutist reading of the interaction of Christ with history.[72] Too much depended upon God's

67. See DWH, 244.

68. Ibid.

69. Ibid., 232–33.

70. What Balthasar presented must be seen as Balthasar's understanding of Barth, and not really indicative of Barth's own position.

71. Balthasar, ET1, 248–49.

72. Thus, as Aidan Nichols explained, Balthasar saw "traces" of idealism throughout Barth's work, and so Barth often had the same kinds of problems generally associated with idealism. That is, idealism was often monistic and Promethean, and therefore, absolutist. Barth strove to overcome this but Balthasar's representation of him suggested that Barth failed to do so when his system is examined as a whole. See Nichols, *Divine Fruitfulness*, 93.

eternal vision and calling.[73] God knew that there would be sin, and yet God also knew he would do something about it. There would be an absolute calling and election of all humanity in Christ, while Christ, being sent away from the Father, would be the one who was to experience the consequence of sin:

> God is obliged in justice to reject sinners, and he must, as God, draw his sinless Son to himself as the first of the Elect. But God will do such in such a way that the Son of God will load all the sins on himself, "even to tasting reprobation, death and hell" (4,179) while sinners —- totally and without exception trapped in their disobedience—are to be set free for the sake of His Son, "so that he might have mercy on all" (Rom 11:32).[74]

Balthasar believed that Barth's God gave mercy to all because of the way sin was put upon Christ. No one will be rejected by God. There is no subjectivity involved here; there will be no need for a subjective experience of salvation, for it is a purely objective reality.[75] Without such subjectivity, freedom was lost, which of course was troubling for Balthasar: he constantly reiterated that such a loss of freedom destroyed one of God's greatest gifts to humanity.[76] Balthasar believed that Catholic theology accepted the general direction of Barth's ideas (as he presented it),—that is, Christ did work for the salvation of all, but Catholic teaching did not systematize Christ's action as being an absolute indication of what will be, because Catholic doctrine took into account human freedom. For Barth, it was merely a system of egress-regress made absolute. "The schema of egress and regress dominates Barth's doctrine of predestination, so much so, as we have seen, that one is in danger of somehow getting 'behind' the curtain of God's judgment

73. See Webster, "Balthasar and Karl Barth," 252.

74. Balthasar, *The Theology of Karl Barth,* 177. [Henceforth, KB]. To be sure, Balthasar liked much of this description, and would use it in his own theology, but he adapted it in a way he believed distanced himself from what he believed were Barth's mistakes.

75. KB, 184.

76. Nonetheless, it must be understood that our freedom is limited; our cooperation with God is what brings us into greater freedom—the more we work with God, the more of that freedom we receive. Humanity, even in its fallen mode of existence, contains some element of freedom, but what is there, independent from God, is not enough to attain what we desire, which can only be the "super-natural" goal of humanity as the experience of the divine life, a goal which elevates our freedom to its fullest possibility. See Balthasar, *Man in History*, 207.

and sneaking a peek at the cards in the Judge's hand."[77] While Catholics, like St. Thomas Aquinas, could also be seen as exploring an egress-regress ordering of salvation history, they resisted making it absolute by the way they took account of human freedom; thus, Catholic doctrine was not to be seen as a "shallow" repetition of the egress-regress schemata but one which transcended it when needed.[78]

The criticism Balthasar gave to Barth is the same kind he would give to any who would teach that all *would* be saved. It is over-systematic and too optimistic. Scripture's presentation of history, especially in the Book of Revelation, does not allow for such a simplistic belief. The Book of Revelation reveals a conflict in history, a conflict which can only end with the fiery judgment of God: "fire descends from God to decide the battle's outcome, and evil's innermost potency is thrown to eternal, self-devouring torment along with the two beasts who are its embodiment."[79] The intensity of the Apocalypse, with its dread warning of the last judgment, serves as a warning against any simplistic *apokatastasis:* there can be no prediction made as to what will happen at the end of the conflict. All that has been revealed is the pattern of the conflict between God's love and its rejection throughout history, a pattern which shows the intensification of that rejection the more God offers his love. What will be in the end of history, if that rejection will continue to the very end, is not known, but those undercurrents of history demonstrate why no conclusion about the end of history and the fate of humanity, let alone of any particular person, can be made. "The final drama has not yet taken place."[80]

HOPE AND RISK

God, in the act of creation, limits his absolute power in a kenotic act which gives room for creation and its freedom. Creation is a Trinitarian act. Just as the persons of the Trinity give themselves completely over to each other, in an act of self-giving love, so God gives himself over to creation in such a way as to make it free to be its own. As Gerard F. O'Hanlon pointed out, this meant for Balthasar that there is a kind of risk God takes upon himself in the act of creation, a risk which is taken into account while creating:

77. KB, 259.
78. See KB, 261.
79. TD4, 42.
80. TD4, 11.

> The lively and dramatic image of a trinitarian God allows sin to affect God without in any sense forcing or dominating him. This is so because within the inner trinitarian life of love there is present the ultimate in self-giving which surpasses and contains all other modalities of love, and so is able to take account of the effects of the refusal of love (the 'risk' God takes in creating us).[81]

God, in the act of creation, grants creatures their freedom. The more God, in an act of love, draws closer to a creature, the more he gives it an opportunity to attain greater freedom, making God risk a greater refusal of his love. This risk is necessary in order to provide creatures the possibility to find their perfect freedom dwelling in the infinite freedom of God:

> Since God is the 'idea' of all freedom and as such is infinite, as Creator he can only create finite freedoms, and they can only thrive by participating in infinite freedom. God sets the limit in order to remove it, so that there may be no barrier between finite freedom and himself.[82]

The freedom God gives to creation, therefore, presents a "risk" to God, for God truly has given creatures the freedom to turn themselves away from him.[83] God's response to such refusal is to attempt to turn creatures back around to himself, not through force or compulsion, but by persuasion.[84] The final act, the eschatological end, represents the ultimate outcome of God's attempt to persuade sinners to return to him. The end result of God's work is not known by those still living in history and have not crossed over and encountered the eschaton. There is hope that in an encounter with God, with God's loving work for the salvation of creation, anyone and everyone could be saved. There is therefore a hope that in the eschaton God will find a way to accomplish his goal, because he has prepared a place for all in himself. "Christian hope, theological hope, goes beyond this world, but it does not pass it by; rather, it takes the world with it on its way to God, who has graciously prepared a dwelling in himself for us and for the world."[85]

Despite such hope, consistently stated that there is the risk that some will continue to turn away from God. Because of the work Jesus

81. O'Hanlon, *The Immutability of God*, 34.

82. TD2, 272.

83. The ultimate risk for humanity is that humans will say no to Christ and yes to Antichrist. See Servais, "Freedom as Christ's Gift to Man," 566.

84. See TD5, 55.

85. TD5, 176.

accomplished on the cross, rejection of God can continue, but now in a greater, more devastating way than before the incarnation.[86] Hope for the salvation of all cannot neglect this tragic possibility. Scripture was clear that there will be a judgment, and that it will be given by Jesus. This is a real, and very dire threat, one Balthasar did not want to whitewash; but he said he did not want to ignore the hope shown in Scripture that Christ could prevail. The two must always exist, side by side, until the God's judgment had been given:

> I only dispute the series of threats invalidates the cited universalist statements. And I claim nothing more than this: that these statements give us a right to have hope for all men, which simultaneously implies that I see no need to take the step from the threats to the positing of a hell occupied by our brothers and sisters through which our hopes would come to naught.[87]

For Balthasar, any attempt to declare what happens in the eschaton is faulty and ignores the freedom which God gave to creation. Apokatastasis is erroneous because it tries to establish a conclusion to history which has not been revealed, and in doing so, it undermines human freedom. Those who criticize *apokatastasis* are therefore correct in rejecting it for its undermining of human freedom. But the other side of *apokatastasis*, the belief that some, if not most, of humanity has already been predetermined to be among the lost, is every bit as wrong as *apokatastasis*. It undermines the freedom God has given to his creatures, and tries to impose upon history the eschaton which cannot be known in history. The only thing available is an agnostic stand as to what happens to the whole of humanity in the eschaton. That alone preserves the freedom which God has given humanity in creation.

IN SUMMARY

Balthasar believed that two different dynamics of freedom had to be preserved by theology. First, God himself is free and he freely gives his love to his creatures. Second, in the act of creation, God gave creatures their own freedom, with the possibility that they could choose to love him and receive his glory thanks to that love, or they could reject him and suffer

86. See TD5, 22.

87. DWH, 187.

the consequences of that rejection. In the fall of Adam, humanity chose to distance itself from God, creating the condition in which it experienced the anxiety and suffering which emerges when they do not find themselves rooted in God. This distance was only the foundation of the continuing encounter between God and humanity; due to humanity's initial rejection of God, God, in the incarnation of Jesus, worked a way to present humanity another chance to say yes to God and to find themselves saved. The negation of God by humanity was met by the response of God to show his love to humanity and to give humanity once again the chance to love him back and to be healed from the consequences of their initial denial of him. Whether or not anyone will do so is up to them and their own personal freely made choice. Because history serves as the continuation of the interaction between these two forms of freedom, between humanity's response to God and God's continued work to persuade humanity to come to him and his saving grace, the outcome of history, whether or not anyone will ultimately deny God's saving love, is not known and cannot be known. The hope must remain that God will persuade all of humanity to accept his love and save everyone, but the fear must also remain that some might contend against God to the very end and so end up among the damned. The hope for the salvation of all as well as the possibility that some might be damned are founded upon the freedom God gave to humanity and this freedom is something that systematic theology cannot override in its eschatological explorations.

III

Dramatic Soteriology

AESTHETIC THEOLOGY AND THEO-DRAMA

BALTHASAR'S UNDERSTANDING OF PERDITION came out of his soteriology. This means that before discussing further his explanation of perdition, his soteriology will have to be explored. To do this, we have to explore Balthasar's notion of a "theo-drama." It is the belief that all of history is a divine drama in which all of humanity is cast to play a part, but Jesus' saving work is the central act of that drama:

> This "theo-drama" is a "theological" undertaking: that is, it reflects upon the dramatic character of existence in the light of biblical revelation. Thus our reflections are themselves *based on* this revelation: they do not merely seek it. This is immediately evident from the fact that our view of God, the world and man will not be developed primarily from below, out of man's "understanding of himself": it will be drawn from that drama which God has already "staged" with the world and with man, in which we find ourselves players.[1]

Balthasar developed the notion of a theo-drama as a result of his theological aesthetics. Drama is what happens after the aesthetics, for the aesthetics shows us how we encounter the glory of God, while the drama

1. TD2, 9.

explains the action which comes from this.[2] Balthasar believed that aesthetic theology was an important foundation for any theological endeavor because it showed us how God's glory is given to us in a beautiful and awe-inspiring form, one which draws us toward God (setting the stage for our participation in a theo-drama):

> The form as it appears to us is beautiful only because the delight it arouses in us is founded upon the fact that, in it, the truth and goodness of the depths of reality itself are manifested and bestowed and this manifestation and bestowal reveal themselves to us as being something infinitely and inexhaustibly fascinating.[3]

Beauty is enchanting. It motivates us. The beauty of God, more than any other beauty, is capable of drawing us in and bringing us to ecstasy. Christian theology, therefore, must not neglect God's beauty; it has to incorporate it within itself. In doing so, it will look at and see how this beauty is diversified in creation, and is capable of being brought into its source, the beauty of God.[4]

The fullness of God's glory is revealed to the world through Jesus Christ. This means that it is in and through Jesus the whole of the Trinity is shown to be at work in the world. "In the one Christ the Father renders witness to himself through the Holy Spirit, and the one Christ, in the indivisible form he sets before us, witnesses to the Father and in the Spirit."[5] The glory of God, revealed through the Son, makes room in the world for all lesser forms of glory. Such lesser glories are justified so long as they are handed over to the Son, Jesus, to be incorporated into him. For the Son is able to embrace the whole world, and enhance it through giving it a share in the divine glory.[6] Thus, as Louis Dupré explained, human culture, with all its glory, has a place in Christ so long as it is not used to keep anyone separated from him.[7]

While beauty can enrapture those who view it and turn them into contemplatives, Balthasar believed that God expected a different response

2. A full exploration of Balthasar's aesthetic theology and theo-drama lies outside of the context of our study here, and should be explored elsewhere. For introductions on each, Nichols's *The Word Has Been Abroad* and *No Bloodless Myth* are recommended.

3. GL1, 118.

4. See O'Donaghue, "A Theology of Beauty," 1.

5. GL1, 154.

6. See Zaborrowski, "*Mythos oder Geschichte*," 57.

7. See Dupré, "Hans Urs von Balthasar's Theology of Aesthetic Form," 300.

from his creation. Everyone is called to interact with him. In this fashion aesthetics is to serve as the foundation for the way God's creatures first encounter him, but then they are expected to act and react based upon that encounter, so that they have a true engagement with God. Ethics, it can be said, flows from aesthetics, for the glory of God revealed in beauty suggests to the creature a way to respond to God, for such beauty makes ethics something other than arbitrary.[8] People can only know the outcome of God's good actions towards them as truth after they have engaged God for themselves, as Balthasar explained: "The good which God does to us can only be experienced as the truth if we share in performing it (Jn 7:17; 8:31f.)."[9] Thus, while God is the central actor of the drama of history, God wants everyone to act with him, to respond to him in order to find their proper place in the order of creation and to appreciate the rightness of that order from within. This means that no one can remain unmoved by God. Everyone is called out of themselves, out of their little corner of the stage of history, to participate in the glorious act of God in Jesus Christ. The drama is all around, and no one is outside of it, and human history is always partaking of that ongoing drama.[10]

While Christ is central to the drama, he brings the rest of creation into it by the way he incorporates all things into himself, showing that all things already have a relative value of their own given to them at their point of origin:

> But this completion of the meaning of history in Christ is not to be understood as though created nature had in it no immanent meaning, no intelligibility, *eidos*, of its own, but only in Christ. Unless the Incarnation involves the acceptance of an immanent essence conferred by the act of creation and able to be lost, there could be no true Incarnation, no possibility of God's becoming man and becoming history.[11]

All that Jesus accomplished in his incarnation, especially his death and resurrection, is the central act of the theo-drama. God had become human, spoke as a man, and revealed himself in the God-man of Jesus Christ.

8. See Kuzma, "Theo-Dramatic Ethics," 28.

9. TD1, 20.

10. See TD2, 63.

11. Balthasar, *A Theology of History*, 114. *Eidos* or form can be seen as the essence of the thing being incorporated.

Jesus is all embracing, for he has taken the fullness of the human condition, as Cardinal Joseph Ratzinger (later, Pope Benedict XVI), explained:

> God speaks as man—this means that God also assumes the manifold self-transcendence of the human word, which as human is embedded as much in man's history as in his nature. God's word, which is pronounced as a word of man, "passes necessarily beyond itself into a total human word" and thus by definition carries with it the cargo of human history.[12]

Everything that is authentically human is embraced by the incarnation. History is embraced by and incorporated into the theo-drama. Balthasar's controversial theology of the descent of Christ into hell must be understood under this paradigm. Nothing can be left outside of the activity of God, and Jesus is the one who reveals that activity to us. The theo-drama shows God is everywhere, making room for everything, drawing everything back to him. If there can be someplace where God is not, God would not be God. The realm of the dead seems to be a place of non-being, of anti-God. Yet God is there. How? Through the descent of Christ into the abyss of death, an event in time and eternity both. It is by his descent into the abyss of death that even death is transformed, so that tragedy can also encounter God's saving grace and the drama does not have to end as tragedy.[13]

Since the incarnation embraces the fullness of humanity, from its heights to its lows, Jesus could make room for everyone to decide for themselves whether or not they will act with him, perform with him, and find themselves united with him for their salvation. The drama is God's drama, and God is present everywhere, making room for all that happens and all that could happen on the stage of creation. It is, nonetheless, important to realize that this means that the theo-drama is, in a way, open-ended. God is at work everywhere, in ways which we do not always understand or see, and this is what gives everyone room to act with him.[14] Everything is embraced by God, not in a way in which the gift of freedom is taken from his creatures, rather, in a way which affirms it.

12. Ratzinger, "Christian Universalism," 547.

13. See Wigley, *Balthasar's Trilogy*, 87.

14. God transcends our ability to try to define him, and so the theo-drama cannot be defined as well. See TD2, 62.

THE EXPERIENCE OF SIN

The theo-drama placed Christ into the heart of the human condition. He embraced everything which is found in history and made it his own, This included, in a very special way, the experience humanity felt in their alienation from God as a result of Adam's fall. The drama had taken a dramatic turn with Adam. By entering creation, the Son comes into it realizing the tragedy which Adam had established so that he can find a way to turn that tragedy around and bring his creation back to him. "The central issue of the theo-drama is that God has made his own the tragic situation of human existence, right down to its ultimate abysses; thus, without drawing its teeth or imposing an extrinsic solution on it, he overcomes it."[15] The theo-drama has Jesus recapitulate the world from within, not from without, to make it new, based upon the structures created by creaturely freedom so as not to impose salvation by some arbitrary act of divine imposition upon it by God. For this reason, what sin did to the world, the suffering it produced in sinners is important; Balthasar believed it was what Jesus himself experienced in his death.[16]

When looking to the conditions the fall placed upon the world, Balthasar saw that humanity had become imprisoned by sin. The human condition was one of alienation from God, where it was incapable of attaining the happiness it desired. Now, this was not to deny free will to a fallen humanity. Its mode of freedom was changed, and in that change, it its freedom became far more restricted, far more limited in its potentiality. Yet, because it continued to have some form of freedom, some of its original potential, there remained after the fall something good and noble; it would be wrong look at everything which was human as something anti-God and to be rejected.[17] Even after the fall, human freedom depends upon

15. TD2, 54.

16. In this way, Christ's cry on the Cross, asking why he had been forsaken, represented a real experience of God-forsakenness which Balthasar believed Jesus would continue to suffer in and through his descent into hell, where Jesus would subjectively feel the effects of sin and the fiery wrath of the Father. This is not to say that Jesus himself was seen as guilty of sin, but rather, he took sin upon himself and felt its effects to the fullest extent possible. While controversial, Thomas White pointed out there were others within the Catholic tradition, such as Denis the Carthusian, who had similar thoughts. See White, "On the Possibility of Universal Salvation," 272.

17. This goes into Balthasar's defense of the *analogia entis*, where he believed that sin did not wipe away the analogy of being from God's creatures. While sin damaged the image of God in his creatures, it did not eliminate it, and where it remained, God could therefore incorporate it in the incarnation. See Donnelly, *Saving Beauty*, 86.

the opening made for it by the absolute freedom of God. The further any would seek some sort of independence from God, the more limited their freedom becomes, yet that freedom, however limited, remains a gift which God has given to all his creatures.

In *Heart of the World,* Balthasar showed how the fall has led everyone to experience the world in an ego-based imprisonment which keeps them alienated from God:

> Prisons of finitude! Like every other being, man is born in many prisons. Soul, body, thought, intuition, endeavor: everything about him has a limit, is itself tangible limitation; everything is a This and a That, different from other things and shunned by them.[18]

Even though finitude — *Endlichkeit*—is experienced as a prison, everyone seems to embrace it because it is what they know. They take that which has been given and try to enshrine it as the center of their being, becoming, as it were, self-enclosed entities who feel shut in by their limitations and yet act as if that finitude were absolute. This is what God wanted to change. Such limitations are not what he intended for humanity. No one needs to be trapped in themselves. They can find freedom beyond their self-made prison if they open themselves up and find their true happiness in God.

When someone seeks to be the absolute in themselves, all they get is their self. The effects of this is expressly made clear in the modern turn to the subject. It makes everyone lonely. Even the sexes find themselves opposed to each other and therefore lonely, as Robert Nandkisore explained, "*Ein Zeichen dieser Zeit ist für Balthasar die Einsamkeit des Menschen.*"[19]Sadly, people have become so accustomed to such loneliness they have grown to accept it despite the suffering it brings to them. Everyone seems to be attached to their egotistical "I," to their self, so that they feel that where it is, what it seems to be like, is what they must promote. If they would do something against this notion of the self, they feel they will lose all they have made themselves to be. So it is this self which forms the existential prison which everyone finds themselves to be in, as Balthasar explained in his meditative discussion with God: "Finally, you yourself have created me to exist within a prison, the prison of my ego. In it I live, move, and have my being. And I love this ego, 'for no one hates his own flesh.'"[20]

18. Balthasar, *Heart of the World,* 19. [Henceforth, HW].

19. "For Balthasar, the sign of the times is the loneliness of man/woman." Nandkisore, *Hoffnung auf Erlösung,* 159.

20. HW, 140.

In the fall, humanity turned inward and embraced itself apart from God. Everyone tried to establish themselves and their limited freedom as being what is absolute. In this way, everyone tried to deify themselves in defiance of God. The freedom they had been given made it possible for them to do this, though, as they found out, the fullness of their desires can never be achieved by themselves. Loneliness shows the consequences of such self-absorption. And yet, despite their experiences, they do not open themselves up to God. Indeed, Balthasar believed that, as a reaction to our existential state, modernity raised individualistic loneliness to a kind of mystical realization, telling us to face with nobility this solitude no matter how painful it is to us. People have come to exalt their solitary existence, embracing the fallen state of being as that which they want to hold onto and not give up. An example Balthasar gave of this was with *Saint-Exupéry* who wanted to show the world that he could thrive in the open space alone as an aviator, high up in the air, leaving behind everything and everyone in an act of solitude.[21] This mysticism of individualistic isolation shows how what is familiar becomes what is comfortable, even if it causes suffering, so that it becomes embraced as the ideal.

While people are free to keep to themselves, if they so desire, the belief that they can exist independent from all others, entirely enclosed in their egos, is a fiction. Everyone depends upon God for their existence, and the freedom they use to maintain their ego has been given to them by and is grounded in God. Everyone owes reverence to God because they exist and have been given their own personal being by him. Original sin, in this way, arises as "infidelity and ingratitude."[22] Humans have ignored that their very existence is itself a gift given to them by God, and so they close themselves off from him, trying to stay true to themselves by being attached solely to themselves. In this fashion, they close themselves off from their proper relationship to God, cutting themselves from all that he would give to them which would truly make them happy. The more they hold on to themselves and deny God, the more they turn away from God, the greater their self-imprisonment becomes, and the more limited their will becomes, as it becomes trapped in the habits of sin. Balthasar wrote how someone might come to realize this in and through their own contemplative reflection:

21. Or those who sought solitude in the desert, such as the example of T. E. Lawrence, could be seen as retreating from the world into their own kind of self-isolation. See Balthasar, *The God Question and Modern Man*, 107–9.

22. GL6, 217.

> Somewhere there exists a bright image of me, an image of what I could have been, of what I am still (but how?) capable of becoming. But these 'ghostly hours' recur more and more seldom, and the enveloping layers of everyday life grow stronger and thicker around me, and gradually the husk turns to flesh and the flesh to husk. I seal myself off to God, and this becomes my usual state—my second nature. Maybe this is the habit of sin, the habit of evil.[23]

Because humanity found itself turned inward, with sinners attempting to establish themselves as their own absolute, they find that self becomes diminished, and so they lose even that self which they thought they had. This is the realization of spiritual death, where claims made for the absolute nature of the independent value of each individualized self are shown to be false. Death is the end result, a death which continues to lead humanity further away from God, suffering even more the impact of such spiritual isolationism. Humanity was made for participation in the divine life, but when this is not possible because of sin, then their beatitude is impossible.

Sin has led people to put their very selves in the place of the absolute. There is therefore no recognition or room for the true absolute, God, in the self-established prison of the sinner. The connection to God which gives happiness and joy is lost. Outside the saving work of Christ, the realm of the dead is where humanity fully encounters the mess which sin has established in creation. The realm of the dead is a chaotic, formless realm, a realm of inactive unfreedom. Outside of Christ's descent into the realm of the dead, the dead found themselves entirely powerless, in the pit death, that is, Sheol. There is no judgment, just isolation. It cannot be said to be hell, for hell emerges from Christ's resurrection from the realm of the dead. For Balthasar, the theo-drama requires Christ to descend into the fullest depths of Sheol so that God could reconfigure the realm of death from within, freeing everyone from the meaninglessness of death, given them the possibility to turn to God and receive the beatitude God desired for them, but this then leaves open the greater possibility of perdition:

> The Pre-Hell remained the proper field of play of the redemptive action. In the light of our remarks above, this whole construction [of later theology which saw the judgment in pre-Christian times] must be laid to one side, since before Christ (and here the term 'before' must be understood not in a chronological sense but in an ontological) there can be neither Hell nor Purgatory– and as for

23. HW, 94.

> a Hell of infants of that we know nothing—but only that Hades (which at most one might divide speculatively into an upper and lower Hades, the inter-relationship of the two remaining obscure) whence Christ willed to deliver 'us' by his solidarity with those who were (physically and spiritually) dead.[24]

The human condition, after the fall, was tragic. Sin left humanity experiencing itself isolated, cut off from God. Christ's work was to overcome this prison, to create an opening in it by which anyone can leave it and return to God. To do this, he had to take on the human condition, and take upon himself the burden of our sin, so that he could reconfigure the realm of the dead and its potentiality by his resurrection from the dead.

LOVE AND TRINITY

The existential imprisonment everyone finds themselves in requires everyone to let go of their self, to die to the self, so that it can no longer have control as to who and what they are. Instead of following the path of indifferent freedom, which reinforces that self-made prison, humans must once again follow the path of love, where they overcome of their self not through a nihilistic rejection of the good of their existence, but in an act of love. The solution is to give the self over to God.

Love is the key to salvation.[25] Love overcomes the self, not through annihilation, but by transcending the prison of the ego. The path of this love is revealed in the Trinity, not only because the Trinity reveals God is love, but also because the persons of the Trinity, in their own self-giving love to each other, have reconstituted creation, giving everyone access to their love, the love which everyone needs to engage in order to be saved.[26] The form of God's love, the revelation of that love, is Christ, who is therefore at the center of the theo-drama. It is from Christ God is revealed to be love, allowing the true nature of love to be known. Through Jesus it is revealed that God acts, not as a power imposing itself on others, but through acts of love which continues to affirm the freedom of creation. God's true sovereignty is revealed in that love, including in and through God's willingness to abandon control over his creatures. "God is not, in the first place,

24. MP, 177.

25. Or, as Christopher Hadley, SJ, explained, "without approach to God in love, there is no participation in God's infinite goodness." Hadley, "The All-Embracing Frame," 43.

26. See Hunt, *The Trinity and the Paschal Mystery*, 123.

'absolute power', but 'absolute love', and his sovereignty manifests itself not in holding on to what is its own but its abandonment—all in such a way that this sovereignty displays itself in transcending the opposition, known to us from the world, between power and impotence."[27]

In what is some of his most challenging and problematic language about God, Balthasar suggested that the Trinitarian persons were radically different from each other: they were, he said, as different from each other as was possible, making, as it were, an infinite distance between them.[28] While this meant that none of the Trinitarian persons could be identified with any other, they were equal and united with each other in the divine essence.[29] Their unity lay in the communion of being, a communion of love.[30] Love unites the Trinitarian persons, and this is what overcomes their radical distinction. The love of the Father could be seen in the self-giving of the Father as he generates the Son, giving everything of himself over to the Son.[31] Likewise, the Son and the Spirit give themselves over, completely and entirely, to each other, and to the Father, so as to also overcome the limitations of self-enclosure. Each of the Trinitarian persons do this so as to bestow upon the others their very selves as a gift of love. This self-transcendence in love, an act of kenosis, allows them to "die to the self," only to get themselves back in a greater measure from their beloved, making their self-giving "death" not something negative and destructive but a

27. MP, 28.

28. "This divine act brings forth the Son, that is, the second way of participating in (and of *being*) the identical Godhead, involves the positing of an absolute, infinite 'distance' that can contain and embrace all other distances that are possible within the world of infinitude, including the distance of sin." TD4, 323.

29. See TD5, 66.

Although this idea of Balthasar is very interesting and with some merit, nonetheless it must not be understood in any way which would lead to the proposal of a Tri-theism. This radical differentiation seems to be almost the reverse of what one found in the time of Athanasius, where differences between the Father and the Son were seen as an Arian teaching. See Pelikan, *The Emergence of the Catholic Tradition*, 209–10.

In this way Balthasar's radical language is troubling, even if he tried to overcome such qualms by the way he expressed the unity within the Trinity. Moreover, as Christopher Hadley also suggested, this leaves open the possibility of reading the Trinitarian kenosis along Hegelian lines, which would overturn the sense of freedom which Balthasar himself wanted to establish, and turn the Trinity not into a Tri-theism but an outright monism. See Hadley, "The All-Embracing Frame," 207.

30. See López, "Eternal Happening," 94.

31. See TD5, 84.

positive "super-death."[32] In this way, Balthasar thought that death did not have to be seen under a negative light; within the Trinity, the "super-death" of the persons of the Trinity form the foundation by which our death can turned into something good.[33]

THE ACCOMPLISHMENT OF CHRIST

The incarnation reveals the Trinity to humanity, showing that God is indeed a God who is love. But this is not the only thing the incarnation accomplished. The Trinity, in Christ, worked for the salvation of creation, allowing those lost to sin to be saved. What was it exactly that Christ did? Balthasar thought that the answer was not easy to give: it involves a great mystery of the faith, and to do it justice, there are many angles which have to be examined in order to give an adequate presentation how Christ rendered God's salvation to sinners.

In the incarnation, the Son reveals the glory of God to those who have turned away from God due to sin. Since they did not see it, since they had turned their backs to it and lost its presence in their lives, they lost the ability to engage it properly. The incarnation made sure no one would remain without some encounter with that glory, so that everyone once again would have to make a response to it. "The lightning-flash of God's glory has struck the earth: eternal time has made its impact felt in the time of men, eternal love has poured out all its blood into the death of a human being, has rested in the irrevocability of Hell, and has 'prepared a place beside the Father' (Jn 14.2) for those doomed to futility."[34] God's glory has been revealed, showing everyone the greatness of God, and yet contained within it are the hidden, transcendent depths of God. The revelation of God's glory truly reveals God to all, but God transcends what anyone can receive. People therefore can open up and receive more and more of that glory, but as they do so, they realize the more they encounter God in Christ, the more God is known to be beyond human comprehension. "God is incomprehensible, and the more he offers himself to our understanding mind, the more incomprehensibility grows."[35] There is always a limit to our comprehension of

32. Ibid.

33. Ibid.

34. GL7, 528.

35. GL7, 318.

what Christ has done. God's glory, which is revealed in Christ, will always be greater and far more amazing than what anyone can say about it.[36]

Balthasar believed there were five things which the New Testament established as to how Christ worked for the salvation of humanity. Each, he believed, had to be included in soteriological explorations for them to adequately present what Christ had accomplished in the incarnation.[37] Balthasar understood how difficult this has been for theologians throughout the centuries, with even the best theologian often failing to do so, allowing other theologians to pick up what had been left out and to explore those themes to make sure they were not lost to the Christian theological tradition.[38] What were these things Christ accomplished? In a succinct summary of them, Balthasar wrote:

> (1) The Son gives himself, through God the Father, for the world's salvation. (2) The Sinless One 'changes places' with sinners. While, in principle, the Church Fathers understand this in a radical sense, it is only in the modern variations of the theories of representation that the consequences are fully drawn out. (3) Man is thus set free (ransomed, redeemed, released). (4) More than this, however, he is initiated into the divine life of the Trinity. (5) Consequently, the whole process is shown to be the result of an initiative on the part of divine love.[39]

The second of these accomplishments was significant for Balthasar's own theological reflection. He believed that many attempted to explore the way Christ substituted himself for sinners through the notion of solidarity, which, though important, did not go far enough in explaining what Christ had done: Christ had to be more than in solidarity with sinners, he had to atone for their sins.[40] Balthasar acknowledged and respected, as far

36. Indeed, Balthasar would suggest that theology must start with a sense of awe, encountered in silence, before it explores God through praise. See Nielsen, "Depicting the Whole Christ," 30–31.

This means that theology comes out of the silence as doxology, showing that there is indeed something which can be said, but always with the caveat that what is left unsaid is greater than what can be said.

37. See Birot, "'God in Christ, Reconciled the World to Himself,'" 265–66.

38. See TD4, 317–18.

39. TD4, 317.

40. It should not be surprising that Balthasar highlighted Anselm as a theologian whose insights needed to be better appreciated in modernity. See Babini, "Jesus Christ, Form and Norm of Man," 451–52.

as they went, the work of those theologians who reflected upon Christ's solidarity with sinners. "It is very persuasive, in that what was previously formulated in primarily ontological terms is now put in terms of personal consciousness: in Jesus, God himself wishes to share fully in the human destiny; he desires to be there 'for' man."[41] The problem is that they stopped with solidarity and did not show what Christ did for us in such a way as to show how such solidarity with sinners did more than share in their experiences, that is, they did not show how such activity worked for our salvation. There must be some sort of exchange taking place between Christ and sinners, so that Christ can take upon himself the burden of sinner, if his work is to be seen as soteriological. "In reality, it is a question of a gathering together, a concentration of universal sin in Christ: '[God] made him to be sin who knew no sin, so that in him we might become the righteousness of God' (2 Cor 5:21)."[42]

Why did Balthasar find himself so concerned with discussions of solidarity? It was a term he often used in his own writings to reflect an aspect of what Christ had achieved, so he embraced the concept, but he feared that many, like Schillebeeckx, abused it by making it the limit of their theological reflection.[43] As Antoine Birot pointed out, Balthasar understood that this happened because the idea of "sacrifice" has been rejected by modernity, and so theologians scrambled to find something they can turn to, with solidarity being what they picked up for their reflections.[44] If all that could be said is that Jesus thought of himself as going into solidarity with the sinner, then there is no indication that Jesus did anything to save others. To fix that, with any discussion of Christ's solidarity with sinners, there also needs to be a discussion of the ontological accomplishment of Christ.[45] Moreover, he wanted to make sure his readers did not read his discussion of Christ's solidarity with the dead as indicative of ignoring Christ's actual accomplishments in his death and resurrection.[46]

41. TD4, 267.

42. Balthasar and Speyr, *To The Heart of the Mystery of Redemption*, 24.

43. See TD4, 271.

44. See Birot, "Redemption in Balthasar," 273.

45. See TD4, 273.

46. While he embraced traditional theology, he did not want to repeat what was said, but to take the good in the approaches to soteriology he found throughout Christian history. He believed most representations of Christ's work were unbalanced and missed something, so modern soteriologies with their emphasis of solidarity, can serve to show one aspect of what they left out of their thinking. Nonetheless, to ignore what traditional

Salvation, therefore, was made possible because Christ actually put himself in the place for sinners, establishing a true substitution for sin. He was the perfectly obedient lover of the Father. He reconfigured the world and made it new through his work in the world.[47] To accomplish this, Christ willingly died on the cross and descended into the realm of the dead, so that he could actually unite himself with the dead and bring the dead back to life with him through his resurrection from the dead.[48]

Christ, Balthasar explained, went all the way down to the uttermost depths of hell—to the point of non-being, to the edge of the void which is the second death, experiencing all that could be experienced in such a descent.[49] This meant that Christ went further to the edge of being than anyone else, making his activity the only one which encompassed the whole of creation. In this regard, Balthasar explained that Christ saw what no one else did: "But you will encounter something else which man does

---

soteriology had established would tip the scale in the wrong direction, rejecting the basic foundations of Christian understand of what Christ had achieved. See Nichols, *No Bloodless Myth*, 160–62.

In this way, Balthasar could and did find reasons to criticize even what significant theologians, like St. Thomas Aquinas, had written, because they ignored the full ontological significance of Christ's reconstitution of creation in himself. He believed that St. Thoma was focused on the economic Trinity and so did not understand how the immanent Trinity was at work in Christ. "He finds St. Thomas' soteriology lacking because it confines the effects of Christ's passion and death to the economy." Mansini, "Balthasar and the Theodramatic Enrichment of the Trinity," 508.

Balthasar believed that what was revealed in the economy of salvation had real implications for the immanent Trinity, and anything which limited the work merely to the economic Trinity failed to grasp the work of the Trinity in our salvation. Interestingly enough, he had a similar complaint with Luther. See Levering, "Balthasar on Christ's Consciousness on the Cross," 575.

47. See Schumacher, "The Concept of Representation in the Theology of Hans Urs von Balthasar," 60.

48. As an analogy to understand what Balthasar's theology suggests, consider a dead sinner to be like a wounded, person stuck at the bottom of a deep, dark pit. Their wounds made it impossible for them to exert themselves to climb out of the pit. If someone came by, saw the person in the pit, they could go down into the pit, tend to the wounds of the person, and then put the person on their shoulders, if the person so desired. It would be too difficult to climb up out of the pit with the person on their back, but if someone else came around and lowered some rope, then the would-be savior could put the rope around himself and the wounded person, making the two as if they were one, so they can be lifted together by the rope. Thus, Balthasar suggested Christ descended to the bottom of the pit so that everything in it could be put upon him and lifted up with him in his resurrection.

49. See Nandkisore, *Hoffnung auf Erlösung*, 128.

not himself see: the void. The lack of love. The incalculable and inseparable deficit of that goodness which God intended for him."[50] This allowed Christ to see from experience what sin is, in a way no one else could, noting how minute, miniscule, and indeed, petty, sin is in itself.[51]

Balthasar understood the difficulty that many of his readers could have with this presentation. Yet, Balthasar pointed to theologians like Nicholas of Cusa whom he believed could confirm some of the most challenging aspects of his theology. Christ suffered like no one else in order to prove his complete obedience of and trust in the Father. Following Nicholas of Cusa's cue, Balthasar wrote of Christ's obedience indicating how it transcended the obedience of anyone else: "naturally, this is an obedience that lies beyond the limits of what is possible to man upon earth, as the most absolute proclamation to the world of God's disposition of love."[52] This made Jesus the "true possessor, through his own experience, of what 'Hell' means in the New Testament; he becomes the judge who has measured out all the dimensions of man in his own experience, and now can assign to each his lot eschatologically."[53] By surveying the realm of the dead, by going to its limits, Christ has made sure no one and no place finds themselves outside of his activity in the theo-drama.[54]

Yet, as Balthasar, made clear, he did more than survey being. Christ felt and experienced the fullness of sin and the way it alienates humanity from God.[55] This meant that he took the full judgment of sin upon himself. He took the sin of humanity and carried sin itself to the edge of being, to the outskirts of the abyss which he surveyed, where he was able to find the proper place for it. Then he was raised from the dead, allowing him to offer everyone a share of his new life, a share in the resurrection, in exchange for the sin he took upon himself. Christ has become the authority who holds

50. HW, 106. The German was inserted from the original. *Leere* can mean "void," but it can also mean "emptiness," a point which could be intriguing for any Buddhist-Christian engagement of Balthasar's thought.

51. HW, 106.

52. GL7, 232 (he referenced Book 10 of Cusa's *Excitationes* to justify his point).

53. GL7, 233.

54. While controversial, we can see others, including Pope Benedict XI, hint at such a view of Christ's descent into the dead: "The true Bodhisattva, Christ, descends into Hell and suffers it in *all its emptiness*, but he does not, for all that, treat man as an immature being deprived in the final analysis of any responsibility for his own destiny." Ratzinger, *Eschatology*, 216.

55. See Birot, "Redemption in Balthasar," 283–84.

judgment over all who come to the realm of death. He comes to all the dead, not only with God's judgment of sin, but also with God's merciful love. Both are real and are a part of what he brings to the dead::

> His judgment will be the judgment of the Redeemer; yet it will not be a mere phantom judgment, but it will take place as the utterly serious mandate he has received from the Father, in the full truth of the 'Day of the Lord.' The fact that he judges us and does not abandon his judgment means that we belong to him in life and death, that he has power over our eternity, that, in his most just decision, he can place us on his right or left, can call us into his Kingdom or turn us away into the eternal fire. All fear and hope tend toward him, the Redeemer and the Judge.[56]

Because of what he did, Jesus can offer everyone the grace they need to be released from the self-made imprisonment of sin. In death, he made sure that no sinner would be left alone outside of his influence, even though, in their self-embracement, they had sought to remain true to themselves in isolation: "the sinner who wants to be 'damned' by God now rediscovers God in his loneliness—but this time he rediscovers God in the absolute impotence of love. For now God has placed himself in solidarity with those who have damned themselves, entering into nontime in a way we could never anticipate."[57] The prison which sinners have established for themselves has been broken through by Christ. How they react to that encounter him will determine their eschatological fate.

The resurrection of Christ is the eschatological moment when creation finds itself fulfilled. Indeed, Balthasar suggested that creation itself is grounded upon, and established in, the resurrection. "One can say, therefore, that the entire action of the living God in all ages has had as its goal the Resurrection of the Son, that the completion of Christology found in the Father's act is at the same time the fulfillment of the act of creation itself."[58]

In his death on the cross, Christ objectively took the sin of the world upon himself. He had given himself over to sinners and is loaded by their sin, so that, in his descent into hell, he could take that sin all the way to the lowest part of hell and discard it for them.[59] Christ has, in this way,

56. Balthasar, *God Question*, 140.

57. ET4, 422.

58. MP, 205.

59. See TL2, 356.

This goes to show that with Balthasar, there is no concept of an empty hell, for there is

objectively redeemed all things. But Christ also gives everyone free will, and does not force anyone to accept salvation. Everyone is given a choice, and it is in the light that of this choice that eternal perdition in the popular sense becomes possible:

> In the rising from the dead, Christ leaves behind him Hades, that is, the state in which humanity is cut off from access to God. But, by virtue of his deepest Trinitarian experience, he takes 'Hell' with him, as the expression of his power to dispose, as judge, the everlasting salvation or the everlasting loss of man.[60]

Jesus, Balthasar said, left the realm of the dead behind, but he takes hell with him, because, as Balthasar will explain, hell, eternal perdition, is the risk which comes from his soteriological work. Without his descent into the dead, no one would be saved, but with it, there is the chance that some will take the judgment without mercy.

GRACE

Balthasar's understanding of the work accomplished by Christ is incomplete without at least a cursory examination of Balthasar's theology of grace. The restructuring of the order of creation created an opportunity for the salvation of all, but God gave everyone free will, and so the objective dimension of Christ's accomplishment cannot be seen outside of anyone's subjective reaction to it. Grace provides the means by which the two dimensions, that of objectivity and that of subjectivity, can come together and meet.

Balthasar, while possessing notions about grace, did not systematically present a theology of grace in his works. Aidan Nichols noted that Balthasar most often discussed grace, not in the terms of positive theology declaring what it is, but through apophatic theology explaining what it is not.[61]

---

something which is placed here; indeed, even those who are saved really lose something due to their sins, as Lösel pointed out, "Individual sins do not affect their agent in an accidental way. Rather, they affect the very substance of a person. With every sin the sinner loses a substantial part of him- or her-self, which gets disposed into hell. Thus even justified sinners who enjoy eternal beatitude in heaven have given a part of themselves to hell." Lösel, "A Plain Account of Christian Salvation," 152.

60. MP, 177. According to Oakes, this differentiation between "the abode of the dead" before Christ and "hell" or "eternal perdition" finds itself set up in the theological tradition by Augustine. See Oakes, "'He Descended Into Hell,'" 227.

61. See Nichols, *No Bloodless Myth*, 79.

A foundation for Balthasar's notions of grace can be seen in the works of his friend and mentor, Henri de Lubac.[62] That is, Balthasar saw that grace and nature were always inter-related, with the original intention of God was to have humanity freely rise up from its initial, graced creation into participation in the divine life. Creation was itself an act of grace. Everyone was created through grace with a good nature and a potential to open up and encounter God and receive a greater share of being than what they had at their point of origin.[63] Everything here shows that God is the one who takes initiative, not only in creating humanity, but in offering it his grace:

> Now, true to his nature as God, and especially in his historical revelation, God possesses the full initiative in the creature's relationship to him. It is God who says who he is and how one should properly relate to him. For these reasons, in the creature's primary aprioristic structure, which the grace of revelation then draw out to light and brings to its own full reality, passivity has precedence over activity.[64]

In this way, the creature's own "ontological truth," their "essence," was established by God, and he also showed his creatures what it was he intended them to be.[65] This idea is Christological, because God established humanity by the Logos; everyone was formed by Christ and find their personal identity as something which exists in and through him.[66] Christ is the concrete universal, who takes on himself, in his personal history, the whole of creation, becoming not just its creator, but the one who is able to take it all and bring it to its proper and ultimate end.[67] While the whole of the Trinity created the world, the world has a particular place in existence because of the work of the Logos: the space of existence is established by the kenotic act of the Logos in the incarnation, giving the Logos a central role in the formation and creation of the world. The drama of salvation exists in the space made by Christ, the space affirmed by the Father through the Spirit, the space of history itself:

62. See Balthasar, *Engagement with God*, 68–70 for Balthasar's nod to his mentor's *Surnaturel*.

63. See Johnson, *Karl Barth and the Analogia Entis*, 207–8.

64. GL1, 245.

65. TD1, 59.

66. See Scola, *A Theological Style*, 46.

67. See Yeago, "Literature in the Drama of Nature and Grace," 91.

> Within this space man is free to make history happen. But since this space belongs to Christ, it is in no sense an empty space but one that is shaped and structured and completely conditioned by certain categories. The framework of its meaning is constructed of the situations (the interior situations) of Christ's earthly existence. Man cannot fall out of this space which is Christ's, nor out of the structural form created by his life.[68]

Grace and nature are united by the work of Christ, who not only gave his creatures their particular natures, but also the grace that allows them to fulfill God's greatest desire for them, that is, their theosis.[69] Balthasar pointed out that creation was done in the light of such hoped for theosis, that creation itself was done in the light of the recreation which would be achieved by Christ:

> When the word of God goes forth, the creature is given insight into God's purpose in creation and realizes something entirely new: God undertook that first communication of his being, whereby finite, self-aware, free beings were created, with a view to a "second" act of freedom whereby he would initiate them into the mysteries of his own life and freely fulfill the promise latent in the infinite act that realizes Being. This "second" act does not need to be temporally distant from the first: the final cause, since it is the first and all-embracing cause, includes all the articulations of the efficient cause—that is, the world's coming-to-be and God's becoming man.[70]

In this way, grace, or the supernatural element, is itself not separated from nature, while nature itself is not lost or absorbed by grace. As Angela Scola said, "The supernatural is a whole which implies the natural as an ingredient endowed with its own autonomous constitution."[71] What Balthasar considered was not any supernatural order empty of concrete content, but the supernatural order established by the cross. "For every claim of nature is short-circuited by the Cross of Christ. It is only from the Cross, the death of Christ, that the seed of nature can come to fruition in grace. There is no

68. Balthasar, *Theology of History*, 71.

69. While salvation is often the theme discussed by Christians, Balthasar understood that the end is not merely being saved by Christ, but in participating in the divine life through Christ. "This is the whole intention of God, who wills the *théôsis*, the entrance into the trinitarian life. Redemption is a reopening." Balthasar, *Engagement with God*, 40.

70. TD2, 400–1.

71. Scola, *A Theological Style*, 48.

such thing as a direct, unbroken, undialectical fruitfulness in nature that would have immediate bearing on the realm of grace."[72] Grace comes to humanity through Christ, through the cross, making the cross stands at the center of any talk about grace and salvation.

Faith motivates his creatures to open up to Christ, to let him transform them so as to receive grace, as Stephen Fields explained:

> Faith reconstitutes the human person according to its object, Christ, the humanly visible, structured form of God's definitive self-revelation. Through faith, human nature becomes transformed so that the intellect is rendered capable of receiving the forms of grace. Moreover, insofar as the intellect is transformed, so are the will, the imagination, and sensation, those subordinate faculties that serve it.[73]

Faith can only be understood as an act of love, which is why Balthasar believed Luther misunderstood what faith for a Christian was meant to be.[74] In this way, faith opens his creatures up to grace and grace brings us into the life of Christ; it is because they freely incorporate themselves into him that they can experience the removal of their sins by his descent into hell. Grace transforms them so that their life, their very existence, is understood only as it exists in Christ. This is what Balthasar believed it meant for the Christian, that is, they have let Christ work his grace in them so that they become the person Christ intends them to be in him:

> It is the essence of Christian grace that it places the individual in particular christological situations. Grace is not an indefinite ontological Something wanting to be given definitive quality by encountering man in his historical situation. It is not man who defines indefinite grace, but grace which determines man, grace determined by the Father through the Incarnate Son in the Spirit. Man, in himself, is something indefinite, something that is by rights indeterminate, and it is grace which defines him so as to be what he is here and not meant to be, before God, in the Church and in the world.[75]

There can be no discussion of grace without some exploration of the sacraments, the ordinary means by which Christians receive such grace.

72. KB, 387.

73. Fields, "Balthasar and Rahner on the Spiritual Senses," 226.

74. See Howsare, *Balthasar and Protestantism*, 66–67.

75. Balthasar, *Theology of History*, 73.

The sacraments offer Christians many different access points by which they can enter into the life of Christ.[76] They make Christians live out their lives as lives incorporated into Christ, working with him in the world. Baptism allows them to openly participate in the death of Christ so they can be raised up with him to the heavenly kingdom.[77] The Eucharist brings Christ to them, having Christ incorporate himself within their own internal being, so that it is not just that Christians dwell in Christ, but Christ dwells in them. The Eucharist is also connected to Christ's sacrifice on the cross, where he opens himself up to everyone, allowing them the means by which he can take their sins and provide them in return a share of his glory.[78] The Eucharist draws believers together, so that their whole lives can engulfed in the sacramental participation of Christ's accomplishment on the cross.[79] Moreover, the sacrament of the Eucharist is for Christians living in history, bringing to them in hidden forms the grace which will come to them in an unveiled form in eternity.[80] Each of the sacraments, in their own way, brings graces to those who are receptive of them; they open people up to Christ and his work. Through them, not only Christ, but the Holy Spirit, is able to be at work in them, bringing the grace they need in order to be transformed into the people God desires them to be.[81]

Grace is freely given by God and liberates the one who freely accepts it, giving that receptive person happiness and joy, but those who reject grace will find themselves under a greater, more oppressive burden. Grace is offered, objectively, by God, allowing everyone the subjective choice to accept or reject it. Such denial, Balthasar believed is based upon egotistical pride:

76. See TD5, 134.

77. See ibid., 137.

78. See ibid., 134–35.

79. See Balthasar, *New Elucidations,* 120.

80. "The most that can be said is that the Lord's eucharistic time is 'limited' for the individual by his death, and for the whole Church by the Last Judgment. But even that it is not that anything will be withdrawn or cancelled, it is only that this *form* of encounter will have become superfluous, because the Lord will no longer need to give himself under the veils which have been instituted for this part of time, which is the time of the Church." Balthasar, *Theology of History,* 99. This means that for those who might not have received communion while on earth, they will still be able to receive and participate in it in eternity, rendering Christ's words which say everyone must receive it to have eternal life to be valid. The form of that reception might change, but the reality does not.

81. See Nichols, *Say It Is Pentecost,* 176–78.

> Grace, however, must not only be freely given, it needs to be freely accepted, through a certain influence on the recipient by the same grace. Even at the purely human level, it is the case that a freely given grace can bring happiness and liberation to the one who receives it, but, if the latter is proud, he can be humiliated and oppressed by it. In the former case, the recipient's liberated freedom unites with the freedom of the proffered grace; in the latter case, paradoxically, the one who refuses grace, which (alone) could bring them fulfillment, tries to be free and self-fulfilled and fails.[82]

The more a person accepts grace, the more they find themselves becoming the person God intended them to be in Christ. The Christian experiences this as "the progressive growth of one's existence into Christ's existence, on the basis of Christ's continuing action in taking shape in the believer. . ."[83] Someone is said to be "in grace" so long as they follow after and accept such grace according to the standard God established for such acceptance, which includes the realization of its need, that everyone is indebted to God for their creation, for the continuing of their being, and for becoming the person God intended them to be.[84] Someone falls out of grace when they no longer accept God's call to them but instead turn inward and think they can accomplish everything in themselves:

> The creature is not "in" grace, grace is in fact withdrawn, when it refuses this fundamental act, when it endeavors to rest content with the freedom it has received and even to regard this freedom as originating in itself, imagining that, in virtue of its transcendent structure, it can open up the realm of self-transcendence through its own efforts.[85]

The refusal to accept God's grace is an act of self-glorification, an attempt to create one's own self-definition outside of the one God has already given them:

> The more man tries to replace or combine his grace-given *eidos* with some *eidos* invented by himself, the weaker, paler, and more negative becomes whatever he makes of his life. The less what takes shape in this world grows from the basic pattern of Jesus Christ,

82. TD3, 35.
83. GL1, 224.
84. See TD2, 314.
85. TD2, 314.

> the more it consists of mere "wood, hay and straw" which will be destroyed in the eschatological fire of judgment (1 Cor 3:12–13).[86]

Grace opens people up to be transformed, to become the person God intended them to be. It does not force, rather, it encourages people to follow through with God's intention for them, to help them work in unison with God's will for them.[87] Its rejection is the attempted usurpation of God's intention by the creature, to establish a form for themselves which is far different from God's intention for them. This other form, this form established outside of grace, is what will be judged by Christ.

When a creature accepts grace, it means they allow the objective work of Christ to enter into them and transform them from within, to let Christ make of them as he will so that they will become the person he intended them to be and will be welcomed into heaven. To be in grace is to be in Christ, to enter into the kingdom of heaven in Christ.[88] This means that the denial of grace leaves someone without a way into heaven, and so, as long as they deny it, as long as they close themselves off from it, there is no entry into beatitude.

IN SUMMARY

For Balthasar, creaturely freedom was an important theme. God established creation so that his creatures could freely open themselves up to him and receive his grace. God hoped that his great glory would draw his creation to him. They did not. They turned away from him and sinned. While sin hindered this objective, God, in Jesus Christ, worked with his creation so as not to allow such sin to have the final say. He lived and died and suffered the full effects of sin, taking on himself as it were, the sin of the world. He opened himself to the sin of the world, so people could divest themselves of their sin upon him. Once they loaded Christ up with their sin, they found themselves once again able to open themselves up in love to receive God's grace. Nonetheless, to continue to receive that grace, people need to freely allow themselves be transformed by Christ and to become the person God intended them to be in and through their incorporation into the person of

86. Balthasar, *Theology of History*, 123.

87. See Nichols, *The Word Has Been Abroad*, 126.

88. See TD3, 53.

Christ. Any obstruction on their part will close them off from grace, leaving them with their sins.

IV

The Judgment of Christ

THE POSSIBILITY OF PERDITION

BALTHASAR BELIEVED THAT CHRIST'S passion and resurrection created the means by which eternal perdition, hell in the colloquial sense, was rendered possible. In his death, Christ found himself in the heart of the chaos of the abyss, sustaining it, giving all that is anti-divine a place in which it could exist, paradoxically, in and through the divine. Or, as Rowan Williams explained, "God must be such as to make it possible for the divine life to live in the heart of its opposite, for the divine life to be victorious simply by 'sustaining' itself in hell."[1] For Christ's death and resurrection changed what happens to the dead. Death was not the eschaton: Christ himself had revealed himself to be such, so that all, when they die, encounter not just the chaos of death, but Christ who comes to them as their savior and judge.[2]

All who die will encounter Christ, encounter him who comes to them with his love, but also with his judgment of sin. The encounter with Christ is an encounter with Christ as the loving judge. Everyone will be judged. It is possible, in that judgment, some will become eternally lost. The damned,

1. Williams, "Balthasar and the Trinity," 38. That means, "the identity of God appears as a free and loving self-differentiating, a totality of giving so radical that God's giving energy generates *that which it is not* and lives wholly and unreservedly *in* that which it is not." Ibid., 39.

2. See Sara, "*Descensus ad Inferos*," 554.

if anyone truly ends up being damned, would remain in the structure given form by Christ's descent into hades, that is, in hell. Christ made hell a place where all that is anti-God can be for "eternity."[3]

Christ discarded all that is sin in hell. The cross was the means of God's final judgment of God over sin, where God's fiery anger expels sin to the remote depths of the abyss.[4] Though this judgment takes place on the cross, it needs to be applied to creation. This is what happens when we are judged by Christ. He comes with the authority to adjudicate the fate of all the dead, where his soteriological action is applied to all: he takes all that is sin in us and casts it into the abyss, freeing sinners from their sin. For those who willingly let this happen, this judgment becomes a purification process, but for those who want to keep their sin and identify themselves with it, they shall be cast down with their sin and become lost with that sin.

What this suggests is that Christ's objective work to save everyone requires their cooperation with him for it to be rendered effective. They must go through Christ's judgment, his keen examination of who they are and where they have sinned, so that he can take that sin from them, free them from its burden, and then lead them back to God. He sees all, knows the thoughts and desires of all, and knows what they have done; this is what makes Christ the proper judge of all.[5]

Christ is the judge and his judgment is real. It will not be an easy experience to go through; his judgment is something to be dreaded. Before they are saved, sinners must accept Christ's judgment upon them, which will then allow Christ to convert them from what they had made of themselves in their life to what God would have them be. This is one area where

3. See TL2, 326. Balthasar understood that this could be seen as troubling: hell, because it is the place in which all that is sin is discarded, ends up being self-contradictory in essence: "there is a contradiction in the essence of hell itself, insofar as hell is discarded sin. Hell is and at the same time is not. Consequently, it is ultimately something that is at once atemporal-eternal and self-destroying, perishing, 'dragged down', 'eddying down.'" TL2, 351.

Much of what Balthasar said on hell can be found bound by this internal self-contradiction, allowing for paradoxes which are difficult to resolve, making what Balthasar says in one place often appear to contradict what he says someplace else. It comes, in part, because system building on the eschaton is impossible, and this is just one example of that impossibility. It is clear he wanted to follow orthodox prescriptions, and so he took it for granted they were to be seen as a part of the whole, but how successful he was able to present this is open for debate, and can only be discussed when his discussion on perdition is fully explored.

4. See Sachs, "Current Eschatology," 240.

5. See Balthasar, *Does Jesus Know Us*, 41.

Balthasar's thought becomes very tricky. He will describe the subjective dimension of the sinner during Christ's judgment, making it appear as if there is a conversion going on after death, with no relation to what the sinner did in their lifetime. This is not what Balthasar intended. He believed that there is no after-death conversion in that sense. Whatever allows for the sinner to accept the judgment of Christ and say yes to him comes from what they have done with grace before their judgment by Christ. In death, a sinner will realize the conversion which was taking place during their lives, surprising them, as it were, with the fact that they had, in the deepest recesses of their heart, already said yes to God. This fits the surprise Christ himself gives to the saved in the parable of the last judgment (cf. Matt 25: 31—46). Balthasar made the point that the process by which this yes to God is revealed will not be pleasant, for it requires the removal of all the layers of sin which hide that yes, which is why the one who is to be saved will not realize the grace they have within until their judgment by Christ. It only after all the layers of sin is removed from a person will they be able to see what grace, if any, they allowed to be seeded within them to allow for their transformation in Christ.

For Balthasar, there are three important points which had to be said about the judgment Christ. First, everyone will be shown who and what God intended them to be, that is, what role God intended everyone to have in his theo-drama. Second, everyone will be judged based upon those expectations; where those personal expectations are not met, there will be sin. Certainly, God allowed everyone to have some flexibility, some creativity in the way they acted upon the role given to them, but when that creativity goes astray, there God by rights has the authority to denounce us and reject them. Thirdly, the outcome of the judgment will depend upon how someone responds to Christ's judgment. That is, Christ will judge and show the sin, show the person how they failed to become the person God intended them to be, but he is doing more than that, he is offering his saving grace to those who accept this criticism and allow Christ to transform them into that person which they failed to be. Christ will seek to remove all that is sin from everyone as he encounters them in the judgment, but he does not force that separation of the sin from the person who sinned. The question then is will they allow Christ to make the separation for them or will they resist Christ? What happens in the judgment will come about as a result of how someone had already interacted with grace during their lives. If there is some element of grace, some acceptance of God's condemnation and mercy, already active, this will be brought out and help the person being judged to fully accept Christ's pronouncement and be freed from sin. If there is not, if someone has entirely cut themselves off from all grace, then there will be nothing inside them which will bring out that yes to Christ, and so they will end up stuck in their no to God forever.

The judgment keeps Christ at the center of the theo-drama, but it also points out that everyone's place in the drama of history is important to God. It is what they do which reveals who people are or what they have become. By making a space for human activity, the activity itself is what is important. It is what is done in history which is judged by Christ, and so it is in history when people reveal who they are in relation to each other as well as to God. Thus, as D.C. Schindler elucidated, "According to Balthasar, the fundamental purpose of the theater in world history has been not merely to describe one or another aspect of the essence of existence but to reveal man to himself, to display in a concrete image who he is. It does so by presenting man engaged in 'significant action.'"[6] Christ's judgment is then the revelation of history because it reveals to each and every one who and what they are due to their active engagement or active disengagement with God.

THE ONE JUDGMENT

In death, everyone finds Christ is there waiting for them. In death, everyone finds themselves turned toward Christ. He comes to all as their judge. Balthasar, in a rather unexpected way, portrays this judgment as being both the particular judgment, which is expected to happens after death, and the universal judgment, which is expected to happen at the end of human history.[7] That is, Balthasar believed that our particular judgment should not be seen as something entirely separate from the universal judgment, as if they were two distinct judgments. Balthasar's position seems to differ from and depart from the way eschatology has been presented by the Congregation for the Doctrine of the Faith (CDF) in 1979,[8] as well as the International Theological Commission's (ITC) elaborations on eschatology in 1992.[9]

6. Schindler, *Hans Urs von Balthasar and the Dramatic Structure of Truth*, 313.

7. See ET1, 265.

8. See Sacred Congregation for the Doctrine of Faith, *Letter on Certain Questions Concerning Eschatology*.

9. The International Theological Commission (ITC) in 1992 took eschatological questions further than the 1979 CDF letter and pointed out that the church teaches a

How did Balthasar justify a position which seemed to go against the 1979 pronouncement on eschatology?[10]

---

kind of intermediate state between death and the resurrection. "A certain intermediate state of this kind is affirmed in the New Testament insofar as an immediate survival after death is taught as a theme quite different from that of the resurrection—a resurrection which in the New Testament is certainly never posited in connection with death. It must also be added that the affirmation of this survival underscores, as a cardinal idea, communion with Christ," International Theological Commission, *Some Current Questions In Eschatology (1992)*, sec 3.4.

Since the last judgment traditionally occurs at the resurrection, and the resurrection is said to be deferred until the end of time, Balthasar's joining together the particular and last judgments appears to be the kind of theological view which the CDF and the ITC criticized.

10. Before exploring Balthasar's understanding of the judgment, it must be made clear that he understood he was looking at a difficult topic, and he was speculating in a manner which differed from normal presentations of the two judgments. As such, he wanted to affirm what the church affirmed and would not want others to follow him if he made mistakes. The CDF itself also wanted theologians to be free to engage such exploration, even if by doing so, a theological opinion would become a dead end and must be rejected. "There is no question here of restricting or preventing the theological research that the faith of the Church needs and from which it should profit. But this does not permit any omission of the duty to safeguard promptly the faith of Christians on points called into doubt." CDF, *Letter on Certain Questions Concerning Eschatology*. It is often difficult to see Balthasar's views as lining up, on a literal level, with the CDF's pronouncements, but it is clear he tried to deal with those areas of concern and keep to the spirit if not to the letter of their concern. Karl Rahner certainly was another who faced similar criticisms, and it would seem, he transcended the spirit as well as the letter. For Rahner, there was a sense that death brought one not just to the judgment, but to eternity and this was what was meant by the resurrection of the dead. A temporal state was therefore not seen as necessary. Eternity incorporated everything in it as the person existed time and entered into their eternal state. "Resurrection is rather the term which, in the view of man's concrete situation, promises the abiding validity of his single and entire existence. Resurrection of the 'flesh' which man is does not mean resurrection of the body which man has as a part of himself." Rahner, *Foundations of Christian Faith*, 268. The resurrection is the transference into eternity of a historical subject, a subject which has finalized themselves and their own personal meaning. "The historical sequence in human life is uni-directional from the inception of the individual life and its biological death. Through biological death, man achieves his final constitution." Rahner, *On the Theology of Death*, 37.

By having the judgment itself as the point between history and eternity, Balthasar is able to suggest a kind of intermediary state which Rahner does not think necessary. In this fashion, when the ITC came to deal with eschatological questions, Rahner's views (which Balthasar borrowed from) were criticized while Balthasar was praised, suggesting that Balthasar's nuances were seen as sufficient for the ITC and the then head of the CDF, Cardinal Ratzinger. See also Hofer, "Balthasar's Eschatology on the Intermediate State," 150.

Balthasar claimed that the Bible knew of only one judgment, "just as there is only one Day of Yahweh or of Christ."[11] The Old Testament as much as the New presented the day of judgment as universal, in that everyone will go through it, but everyone will face it alone, individually, one on one with Christ, which is what makes it the particular judgment.[12] There will be no one there to help the sinner as they are being judged, no intercession from outsiders allowing them to escape their judgment.[13] While he did not speak of two judgments, he admitted that the one judgment had two different, but related, parts, the particular and private judgment, and the public declaration of its results once the judgment was over (rendering its results universal, and allowing the whole of history and the theo-drama to be revealed in and through the universalization of all the particular judgments).[14]

Balthasar believed that the two aspects of our judgment had become separated and distinct in tradition due to theological speculations based upon questionable theological sources, such as apocryphal writings that were taken in and accepted by many Christians in the early Christian era.[15] While they could have had some value to them, they were pre-Christian, and did not incorporate in them what was revealed in Christ. This means that they did not represent Christian theological categories. Moreover, it could be asked, which of them should be trusted if and when all of them, when looked together, were inconsistent and contradicted each other?[16] This is not to say such apocryphal sources should be entirely ignored. Early Christians were not wrong to look at them; the problem is that Christians did not purify them and what they taught when they contradicted authentic revelation, and so those Christians took up concepts which should have been excised from the Christian tradition. Scripture had to be the authoritative source for understanding eschatology, and Balthasar believed, Scripture only knew of one judgment. While he would agree that theological

11. TD5, 346.

12. See ibid., 349.

13. See ibid., 348.

14. See ibid., 349.

15 See Hofer, "Balthasar's Eschatology on the Intermediate State," 155–56.

16 See TD5, 350–51. The ITC document, "Some Current Questions in Eschatology," agreed with Balthasar that there was no consistent pre-Christian eschatology (4.5) and yet believed that Jewish thought on Sheol and its relationship to Catholic talk about an intermediate state could not be easily dismissed (3.1–4).

speculation is useful and should be explored, when it gravely erred, as it did here, then such errors must be denied.[17]

Why was Balthasar so adamant that there would be only one judgment? He thought the tradition which developed two separate judgments ended up being nonsensical. There would be no reason for a second judgment. What was decided at the particular judgment could not be different from what was decided at a universal judgment. A second judgment would therefore be inconsequential, for the outcome would already be known. "Insofar as the individual has to step forth into his particular judgment, which is part of the judgment of the world, acts of faith are required of him, namely hope and fear. These would not arise in the case of a final judgment that was separate from the particular judgment."[18]

While Balthasar believed that Scripture knew only one judgment, he agreed that there was a universal aspect to it. How could that be possible if our judgment was so individualized and particular? The answer to this riddle, he believed, was given by Rahner: the universal aspect of the last judgment can be found in the fact that there is one judgment happening alongside history, and the universal judgment itself was the summation of all the individual judgments put together.[19] Everyone could experience that universal aspect of their judgment as well, because everyone will see how their actions in time fit in with the whole of humanity. God would show to everyone at their particular judgment his guiding judgments over the totality of human history, giving everyone an understanding of their place in that history, including how their actions have helped or hinder the God's desires for that history.[20] In this way, the universal aspect of the judgment could be said to be the "*summa summanum* of all particular judgments," where the whole of history, collected together, can be seen and understood through "the eyes of God," a revelation which everyone could receive at the end of their particular, individualized judgment.[21]

17. See TD5, 356–57.

18. Ibid., 357.

19. See ibid., 357.

20. See ibid., 358.

21. Ibid., 360.

THE RESURRECTION OF THE DEAD

If Balthasar believed universal judgment happened alongside history, what did he have to say about the resurrection of the dead? He believed that the resurrection was taking place "alongside history."[22]

Death for a creature is the end of their existence in time. Temporal existence has a beginning and an end: it is finite. When someone dies, they are no longer an active member of the ongoing development of temporal history.[23] They are brought to their judgment with Christ, in the state of the dead, in a state which is outside of time. Thus, the judgment itself is not to be seen as connected with time but outside of it, as Geoffrey Wainwright explained: "To the question of the 'timing' of the judgment, there is in fact no simple chronological answer, because judgment always takes place not just at the caesura between life and death but more crucially at the threshold of the Old Aeon and the New—which itself takes place only as a vertical intersection from above into the line of world-time."[24]

When someone dies, they leave temporal existence and find themselves in a new modality of existence, the modality of the judgment. What is this judgment like? Is it, as many think, an encounter with Christ as a soul separated from the body? Balthasar did not believe this question could be given a sufficient answer.[25] Nonetheless, he did say something more about this, because he knew too many eschatological concerns revolved around this issue to leave it without some sort of analysis. Balthasar said that there must be something imperishable in humanity, something which continues to exist, even at death.[26] However, he did not like to consider this aspect of the human person as existing absolutely independent from a body. He found it difficult to imagine souls existing incorporeally in

22. Ibid., 360.

23. See TD4, 95.

24. Wainwright, "Eschatology," 119.

25. See TD5, 358. Here, Balthasar seems to have raised the question of the existence of an intermediate state, where the soul exists without the body. The ITC declaration in "Some Current Questions in Eschatology," suggests that such an intermediate state exists for the one being purified (8.1). Balthasar, in his discussion of the duration of the judgment, seems to leave himself open to accepting this kind of "intermediate" state, as long as it is seen is a state and not a continuation unto death of temporal existence.

26. See TD4, 133. In this way, Balthasar agreed with the CDF when the CDF said, "The Church affirms that a spiritual element survives and subsists after death, an element endowed with consciousness and will, so that the 'human self' subsists." CDF, *Letter on Certain Questions Concerning Eschatology.*

heaven; indeed, he pointed out that traditions suggested not only Mary, but others like John or those who were raised with Christ on his resurrection day, could be seen as having received their share of the resurrection.[27] This helped form the foundation for his notion that the resurrection is happening alongside history. To continue with this, Balthasar pointed out how Jesus, when questioned by the Sadducees about the resurrection, suggested that the patriarchs were alive in him (see Matt. 22:32). That is, Jesus implied that Abraham, Isaac, and Jacob (and so, many others as well) were already sharing in the resurrection, for this is why he could say they were alive (otherwise Jesus' response would not have answered the Sadducees' question).[28]

What is to be made of this? Was Balthasar suggesting, in some fashion, that the patriarchs before Christ rose "before" Christ? No. His point was that death takes everyone out of time and to the point of the eschaton in Christ. The resurrection takes us to heaven, which is supra-temporal, and so the patriarchs, when they died in a time before Christ, nonetheless entered a supra-temporal form of existence where Jesus is to be found.[29] Jesus is the firstborn of the dead, the first who is to be resurrected, that is, he is ontologically the first to experience the new creation in heaven, but he did so meta-historically, allowing for those of the dead in history, having left time in their death, to join in with him in his resurrection even if his resurrection happened at a later point in time.[30]

It can therefore be said that when someone dies, they are taken out of time and come to encounter Christ. This was true for those who came in time before Christ, as it is true to those who come in time afterward. As someone exits time, they enter a state which transcends time and so the qualities associated with time do not properly apply. For the believer, for the one who end up being saved, their death takes them to the resurrection. They become fully incorporated in the eternity of Christ, into his resurrection. "The death of the believer (and, through him, of man generally) is the 'incorporation' of the soul into the heavenly body, heavenly 'temple,' heavenly 'house' of the risen humanity of Christ."[31] To be sure, before this happens, they too have to face the judgment of Christ, which, like the resurrection, outside of time. Jesus, as the one who brings resurrection to

27. See TD5, 358.

28. Ibid., 358.

29. See ibid., 359.

30. See MP, 248–49.

31. ET1, 262.

the dead, has done so for the dead, so that at whatever point in time they died, they come to him, and are able to be brought to the resurrection, even though history itself continues on after their death. This, then, is how Balthasar is able to understand the resurrection as taking place alongside history: history continues, and with it, the exiting of people from history who, if they are saved, find themselves experiencing the resurrection of the dead:

> For the Messiah, who calls himself the Resurrection and the Life, has already appeared in history, and in his dying has reached the end of the world. Not only that: the resurrection of the dead, or their glorification in God, has already begun with his Resurrection and the resurrection of those who rose together with him. And if, as we have shown, the one Judgment can and must take place "along" earthly history, it is hard to see why the same cannot be said of the resurrection, particularly if we keep Matthew 27:51—53 in mind.[32]

Because Balthasar believed it to be difficult to talk about time after death, it is understandable why he has difficulty in talking about the resurrection in relation to temporal categories. Yet, there remains a sense of an intermediary state, even if it is not seen within the domain of time, it is a state of judgment which ends with a universal judgment and participation in the resurrection. In this way, Balthasar solidifies his affirmation of Catholic principles, even if he did so in an unconventional (and not entirely satisfactory) manner. Balthasar did not want to "dematerialize" the resurrection, which is what many, like Cardinal Ratzinger, feared happened with those who posit an immediate resurrection after death.[33] Yet, Balthasar seems to leave open to the kind of paradox which Ratzinger also saw happening with this kind of theological speculation; how can the resurrection and the timelessness of death be affirmed if a person's body remains in history?[34] As long as eschatology and the resurrection are examined using temporal categories, so the resurrection is seen as "afterwards" to world history, these

32. TD5, 360. Matt 27:51–53 said that when Christ rose from the dead, many of the saints also rose with him; thus Balthasar can be seen as to suggest that Scripture itself posits the beginning of the resurrection of the rest of the dead can be seen happening alongside Christ's resurrection. If some are seen to have risen when Christ rose, there is no difficulty in believing others will rise alongside their death, entering into heaven even as earth history continues to move forward to its own conclusion.

33. See Ratzinger, *Eschatology*, 267.

34. See ibid., 252.

questions remain. For Balthasar, the resurrection is not merely an "after" to world history, but the entrance into a new supra-time, which allows history to exist even as the end, the eschaton with the resurrection, exists side by side with it.

THE REVELATION OF THE PERSON GOD MADE US TO BE

How exactly did Balthasar believe the judgment would be made? Christ will show everyone how different they have become as an individual from the person God meant them to be. God has a vision for everyone, a vision which defines who everyone is meant to be. Only God has the authority to make this definition. "Only God can define and designate such a subject in his qualitative uniqueness."[35] Jesus is the central actor in the drama of world history, the theo-drama, and so our authentic persona comes from properly acting with Christ in the theo-drama.[36] The proper identity of each person develops in relation to how we relate to each other in and through Christ. It is in Christ they find themselves not an isolated individual cut off from everyone and everything, but having a real integral part in history, and this part is their mission which then defines who they are to be, as Balthasar explained: "*In Christo*, however, every man can cherish the hope of not remaining a merely individual conscious subject but receiving personhood from God, becoming a person, with a mission that is likewise defined *in Christo*."[37]

No one is thrown into the world without the help needed to discover the persons they are meant to be; everyone is being given direction by God as to what their personhood is meant to be. The theo-drama is Trinitarian in nature. While Christ is the central actor in the drama, the Father can be said to be the author of the drama and the Holy Spirit the one who directs it, helping the everyone find their roles, giving them the freedom to play them out as they see fit.[38] God, in all three persons, is addressing the world,

35. TD3, 220.

36. This, Stephen Ackerman suggested, is the anthropological implication of the theo-drama; personhood only makes sense in relation to the concrete universal of Christ. That is, as Christ is the central actor in the theo-drama, what everyone else is to do in the theo-drama must relate to Christ as the center of history, and so must be derivative from Christ. See Ackerman, "The Church as Person," 241.

37. TD3, 22.

38. See Nichols, *No Bloodless Myth*, 29–32.

calling everyone forth to interact with him. God addresses everyone as the person he intends them to be, and so in this fashion everyone, addressed by God, has that revelation given to them (if they open up and listen). When this is accepted, then truly their authentic personhood is developed and the person can truly recognize that personhood in the mission or call given to them from God. "It is when God addresses a conscious subject, tells him who he is and what he means to the eternal God of truth, and shows him the purpose of his existence—that is, imparts a distinctive and divinely authorized mission—that we can say of a conscious subject that he is a 'person.'"[39]

True personhood is found in relation to the mission God has intended for them in the world, and he will not accept anything which seeks to establish that identity apart from his calling: personhood is "appointed" by God to the person and not created by the person.[40] Being named (or given a new name) by God is indicative of this mission and personhood. Such direction, while established in Christ, comes specifically from the prompting of the Holy Spirit.[41] The Spirit is in the world, sent to it by Christ, to direct everyone so they can find their true personhood in their relationship to Christ. To accept that direction, everyone has to let go of all thoughts or ideas as to who they think they are, they must die to the self, so that the Holy Spirit can then direct and prompt them to become the one God meant them to be. It requires, as Balthasar put it, humility: "And as for the individual, either he would never find his 'person' or he would subsequently lose it and its authentic freedom if he did not have the humility to submit himself to the Spirit's 'direction.'"[42]

In Christ's judgment, therefore, everyone is examined in relation to the person God intended them to be. Everyone will see how they have failed or lived up to God's expectations. Indeed, everyone will be shown their "fundamental choice" in relation to God. This will determine who will be condemned and who will be saved. This fundamental choice, as it has been made in history, is revealed by Christ. It is not a one-time decision made for or against God, it is rather something greater, the fundamental

39. TD3, 207. And so, Babini explained, "By means of the mission received, man discovers why he has been made and who he really is, since it is in mission, received as a gift from an 'other,' that he hears himself called as an 'I' buy a 'Thou,' and (made responsible by this latter) called to a response." Babini, "Jesus Christ, Form and Norm," 448.

40. See TD3, 267.

41. See Wigley, *Balthasar's Trilogy*, 79.

42. TD3, 534.

choice at the core of being, and whether someone has accepted God there or if they have come to a total and hateful denial of the inner prompting of God. It is not an abstraction, but rather, the culmination of what one has made for themselves in life and then revealed by Christ in death:

> This fundamental choice, however, which causes the scales to rise or fall, does not take place *in abstracto* but in the succession of individual life situations; it takes place in a series of acts and stances that are all vulnerable to death and thus constantly highlight the finitude of the area in which this freedom has to exercise its choice.[43]

The judgment is made according to the "quality" and not the "quantity" of that fundamental choice; a person's whole life is seen "relativized to a single moment," but that "moment" is actually a representation of their life in "its totality."[44] Christ will look for any "little seed of love" accepted by the person being judged which is then capable of being used by him to bring them over to him and out of our sin.[45] In this way, everyone will see if and when they have ever been open to God's grace, if and when they have turned away from it, or if they have entirely turned away and rejected it. It is only if there is an absolute and final denial of God which is seen coming from this "fundamental choice," will someone be said to be damned, having established as it were, a wall which divided them from God's love.[46]

If someone has opened themselves to grace, they will be able to open themselves further to Christ in the judgment, allowing Christ to completely transform them into the persons they were meant to be. Grace multiplies itself. Robert Barron's observation about Balthasar's anthropology is in full effect here:

> At the heart of Balthasar's deeply biblical anthropology is the conviction, therefore, that humans are most themselves precisely when they enter into a kind of loop of grace, accepting life from God (who wants nothing more than to give it) and promptly returning it as an act of love, thereby receiving more and more of it.[47]

43. TD5, 295.
44. Ibid., 296.
45. Ibid.
46. See TD2, 314.
47. Barron, "A Reflection on Christ, Theological Mood, and Freedom," 21.

This is why, for the person being transformed, there is a sense of conversion going on, but it is not a conversion in death that is independent from what grace they opened up to and received during life.[48] The judgment is of the person and what they made of themselves in the time they have been given to define themselves by their actions. Time, and the decisions made in time, are real, and they will have an effect in the eternal destiny of each and every person:

> This decision made in time is and remains the basis of his eternity; however much the grace and justice of the eternal Judge might change it and however great the transformation of the condition of the Eon of mortality might be in its transformation to the Eon of immortality, nonetheless, what happens down here determines our status in eternity.[49]

Those who are lost will be those who have closed themselves off from grace so that there is no possibility of conversion to Christ, of transformation to the persons God wants them to be, even though Christ will offer such a transformation to them in his encounter with them.

At the judgment, everyone will be shown, insofar they have followed a path away from God, they have been selfish sinners who did not and do not possess "true love" in themselves.[50] The cross reveals in its light the guilt of all. It reveals to everyone, even if in their fundamental choice they have accepted God's grace, that they have created for themselves a self which is full of sin. It is also in the light of the cross everyone will be shown the abyss of selfishness, of unlove, of Godforsakenness that they have made for themselves and from which they need to be saved if they want beatitude.[51] In this fashion, it is important to make clear, Jesus comes as savior but also judge, and both are united in his judgment. "Thus, both of our eternal lots lie together in his hand: precisely because he is our grace, he is also our judgment; he is our judge and at the same time, our redeemer."[52]

The judgment of Christ reveals to everyone how far they have fallen outside of God's plan for them, but it also shows them the new yes of the Son, the yes of the Son to the Father, which they can join with if they unload their sins, and with them, their falsely constructed notion of themselves,

48. See TD5, 297.

49. ET4, 462–63.

50. See LA, 61.

51. See ibid., 93.

52. LA, 94.

onto him. The light of grace, flowing from the objective work of Christ, gives everyone the chance to accept Christ's judgment, to agree that they have failed God, so as to leave it to Christ to take away their failures. They have to admit their failure for this to happen. They cannot hold on to it. Thus, in the judgment of Christ, not only will everyone be shown how they failed God, they will also be given the chance to free themselves from that failure and be saved. If there be any objective element within a person which continues to reflect God's intentions for them, Christ will be use that as a means to open the person up and receive his grace, the grace which then allows them to put aside the sinful self they created for themselves and become the person God meant them to be:

> The Judgment is the affair of the Son of Man alone (Mt 25.31f.), and it can only take place in the face-to-face confrontation of man with the crucified Lord [. . .] This is a confrontation in which the tough husk of a sinful life will dissolve, while man realises, in an inescapable and inexorable vision, what he has done to Christ, what should have been (and was not) the form of his Christian life, where it is that now, no longer through meritorious but through imposed repentance, he will be melted down and be made pliable for the only form in which he can enter the Kingdom of the Father; this is the "form of Christ" (Gal 4.19), since from now on Jesus Christ will be "publicly portrayed as crucified before [everyone's] eyes" (Gal 3.1). This is the dimension of that judgment which is called 'the purifying fire': the existential event whereby definitive form is given, which should never be forgotten as accompanying the Judge's act of sentencing.[53]

Christ's judgment not only condemns sin, it is a condemnation through the wrath of God, a wrath which puts all that is sin to the fire of God's anger. It is the fiery wrath of God which Christ experienced when he took sin upon himself, a wrath which can become a purgatorial fire if the sinner repents and unburdens themselves upon Christ. Then Christ is seen to become a burnt offering to God, burned by the fire of God's wrath, thanks to his work on the cross. God does not accept sin, and the wrath of God is sent to the sin which Christ takes upon himself. It is able to purify a person and have something remain to be built up, but only if there is something other than sin which is left in the person being judged.[54]

53. GL1, 681.

54. See Sara, "Descensus ad Inferos," 555.

The condemnation of sin reveals God's anger, but it comes as the fiery anger of love scorned. "The love in God's heart is laid bare in all its radicality, showing its absolute opposition to anything that would injure it."[55] Because it is love, it is open to work with the sinner, willing to purify them; the work Jesus accomplished on the cross is the objective foundation for that purification. For it is on the cross that sin is itself judged.[56] If someone does not accept this work, then all they will have is judgment, the fiery judgment of God. "It arises from the inner reality of the grace flowing from the Cross: once a person has refused to accept the gift of grace there is nothing left 'behind' the Cross but the specter of judgment."[57] The love of God requires love in return; only that which finds its place in that love can be redeemed:

> If "God is love" (1 Jn 4:8) his "wrath of fire"(Heb 10:27) can only be the fire of love. But it is so absolute that it burns up everything which is not love. And if the divine love is eternal, this burning must be too. Thus Jesus is not afraid to speak of this eternal fire which devours the enemies of love (Mt 25:41 ff).[58]

What love someone possesses in themselves will not be consumed; indeed, that love, empowered as it is by grace, will not be judged, for there is nothing to condemn about it. In this manner, it can be said to be that part of a person which transcends the judgment.[59]

Sinners must come face to face with God and be judged, whereby they are free to follow through with God's love and be transformed, or to reject it and to be damned. Whether or not they will do so comes from the trajectory of their life before the judgment. What comes forth is the revelation of the yes or no to God within, with any element of yes being made as the basis by which the person is transformed into the person God intended them to be. As long as there is sin, as long as some element of a "no" to God remains mixed with that yes, the person is "unjust," and in need purification. "The unjust man must be brought through a judgment before he can catch sight of God's love and accept it. God would contradict the *rectitudo* of his love if he pardoned a sinner while leaving him in the unjust state in which he finds himself (Anselm, *Proslogion* 9–11)."[60] Condemnation of the

55. TD4, 341.
56. See MP, 119.
57. Balthasar, *Does Jesus Know Us*, 81.
58. Ibid., 82.
59. See GL1, 682.
60. TL2, 142.

sinner ends up being self-damnation, because the sinner does not give in to the loving truth of God's just judgment of Christ.[61] The constant refusal of God's love is the ultimate sin, the unforgivable sin, because the sinner does not allow such forgiveness upon themselves. It is, in a sense, an act of hate against their own being.[62]

Thus the judgment is an apocalypse—a revelation of the soul. Since, as Balthasar wrote early in his life, "eschatology can be defined as the teaching of the relationship of the soul to its eternal fate, whose achievement (fulfillment, alignment) is its apocalypse,"[63] this judgment is eschatological, and indeed, shows Christ to be the eschaton to whom all of us go. In and through Christ we die and come back to life; in and from Christ, we come to God or reject him:

> God is the "last thing" of the creature. Gained, he is heaven; lost, he is hell; examining, he is judgment; purifying, he is purgatory. He it is to whom finite being dies, and through whom it rises to him, in him. This he is, however, as he presents himself to the world, that is, in his Son, *Jesus Christ,* who is the revelation of God and, therefore, the whole essence of the last things.[64]

This means, as Nicholas Healy pointed out, "Christ is the archetype and the accomplisher of the eschatological communion between God and creation."[65] Since eschatology is about the fulfillment of being, so Christ is the center of eschatology; all things in the world move toward him.[66] He reveals his judgment to everyone, and it is their response to his revelation which ultimately leads to their salvation (through purification, which is then their experience of purgatory) or perdition. If, as was said above, they

61. See Ibid., 141–43.

62. See Tourpe, "Dialectic and Dialogic," 318.

63. "Eschatologie läßt sich dann als die Lehre vom Verhältnis der Seele zu ihrem ewigen Schicksal definieren, dessen Erreichung (Erfüllung, Angleichung) ihre Apokalypse ist." Hans Urs von Balthasar, *Apokalypse der deutschen Seele, 4.*

64. ET1, 260–61.

65. Healy, *The Eschatology of Hans Urs von Balthasar,* 91.

66. See ET1, 275. Thus, as Lösel suggested, "Jesus' death and resurrection, which sum up his mission on earth, constitute for Balthasar the end of history, even though the course of time continues. In Jesus' death on the cross, the end of history has come primarily for the incarnate second person of the Trinity. Yet, it also impacts the rest of history: from now on, the *eschaton* directly confronts and newly qualifies history." Lösel, "Unapocalyptic Theology," 208.

reject where Christ would lead them, then all they have is judgment, but if they respond with love, then Christ is capable of leading them to beatitude:

> As the presence of the Word, he is God's judgment; that is, he is 'true light, that (in judgment) gives light to (or illuminates, makes viable) every man' ([John] 1.9), and draws the 'works' of every man to the light (3.19—21); here, it depends on the individual man whether he 'hates' this act of becoming disclosed in the light and then comes into the judgment, or in faith willing lets himself be 'led over' and enters the salvation of the light.[67]

Sinners must let themselves enter into the light of Christ, to follow in faith, obedience, and love, or they will reside in perpetual judgment, in hate, and this is the foundation for their self-condemnation.[68] What happens in the judgment, as has already been said, depends upon the trajectory established in life, whether or not one, in their fundamental option, has opened up to God and grace or denied God and closed themselves off in hate. Because no one knows if they truly have opened themselves to God, to grace, until the judgment, they cannot presume the outcome of the judgment. However, as much as they think they have opened up to God and his love, to the grace of the cross, they have reason to hope they will be saved. For with love, as John Cihak explained, "Even the terrible Day of the Lord can be met in confidence."[69]

JUDGMENT AS INTERMEDIARY STATE

In the ITC's 1992 document on eschatology, the ITC made it clear that an intermediary state between death and the resurrection was necessary in order to explain purgatory:

> In the case of those who have not achieved this adequately by penance on earth, the Church teaches that there is a postmortem purificatory phase, to wit, "a purification preceding the vision of God." Since this postmortem purification is to take place before the final resurrection, it is a state that belongs to an intermediate

67. GL7, 122. When we look to perdition we will take up the theme of perpetual judgment as being what perdition is about, which should explain how this passage fits in Balthasar's schemata.

68. See DWH, 165.

69. Cihak, *Balthasar and Anxiety*, 183.

> eschatological stage; indeed the very existence of such a state shows that an intermediate eschatology exists.[70]

While Balthasar seemed to have questioned such an intermediary state, because of his promotion of the resurrection after death, nonetheless, the judgment of Christ exists between the two, as a state of its own.[71] Balthasar posited such a state, but he seems to want to keep it as a state in flux, and not something which can be measured by objective temporal standards. For Balthasar, purgatory is an authentic doctrine, but it must be understood as a part of the judgment we undergo in death and not something apart from it. "What Catholic theology speaks of as purification beyond the grave must be seen as one aspect of Judgment."[72] The impure confront Jesus and find Jesus purifying them through his judgment. Purgatory is a state, the state of judgment. Everyone finds themselves in the state of purgatory for as long as it is necessary for them to see their sin, agree with the condemnation of it, and then cast it aside upon Christ who is willing to take it upon himself and discard it into the abyss. "Purgatory ends at the precise point where man, looking at the Cross, begins to realize the extent of the world's sin, which somewhere or other contains his own sin. He would have deserved far more punishment."[73]

When someone sees their sin and actually desires to suffer for it, to pay the punishment which is its due, to undergo all that is needed for its removal, then it can be taken away because they are no longer attached to it.[74] The grace of the cross allows this, but this is what happens only for those who end up saved. Those who deny Christ's offer to take away their sin shall be lost in perpetual judgment, where all they will have is their sin and Christ's condemnation of it.[75] They will not abandon it because they are attached to it and think it is what they must hold to, even if it makes them suffer. The judgment shows everyone all that is within them which needs to

70. ITC, "Some Current Questions in Eschatology," 8.1.

71. Because of Christ's descent into the dead, because of Holy Saturday, purgatory came into existence; "before" then, there was no possibility of transformation which would allow one to be raised from the dead. See MP, 178 and Nichols, *Divine Fruitfulness*, 186–7.

72. TD5, 360.

73. TD5, 368.

74. See TD5, 368.

75. We will be receptive of the grace of the cross in the judgment only if our trajectory in life has opened us up to this in our death. Our reaction to the judgment comes in relation to how we have defined ourselves in life and not apart from it.

be rejected, but it is because Christ comes not only as a judge but as a savior, those who accept the judgment are able to be saved. If Christ hadnot followed the path of the cross, there would be no means by which the sinner could cast aside their sin, even if they wanted to.

For those who give themselves over to Christ, then the judgment, however painful it is, melts away their sins so as to make them ready for glorification. Balthasar noted that, following St. Thomas Aquinas, this means that the purgatory and hell share the same purifying fire amongst them. The fire is the same, only the effects are different according to the person encountering it.[76] The fire seeks not to annihilate but to purify, with sin being that which is fuels the flame; the fire continues so long as someone continues to have some sin in them. This means that for those who deny Christ, those who have nothing in them which Christ can use to bring forth a yes to God, all there will be is sin and so all they will have is God's wrath, the constant "now" of God's fiery anger, "a disconsolate immovable now."[77]

By seeing two ways we can interact with their fiery judgment of Christ, Balthasar believed that there would be a difference in the experience of that judgment for those who will end up being saved from those who end up being damned, as the CDF said there must be.[78] The saved will experience mercy which the damned will not. The damned will only know the fire as wrath. However, he thought it must be one and the same judgment which brings about purgatory or condemnation. The source is one, but what was "altogether different" would be the experience of that fire, of whether or not that mercy will be experienced in the fire itself, making for two radically different outcomes (with mercy, it is a fire of love, without it, there is but anger).[79]

76. See ET1, 264.

77. DWH, 133.

78. "She believes that there will be eternal punishment for the sinner, who will be deprived of the sight of God, and that this punishment will have a repercussion on the whole being of the sinner. She believes in the possibility of a purification for the elect before they see God, a purification altogether different from the punishment of the damned. This is what the Church means when speaking of Hell and Purgatory." CDF, "Letter on Certain Questions Concerning Eschatology."

79. The difference is not only teleological, but also, substantial in the sense that those who end up among the saved have an element within which is not entirely "put on fire" and condemned; those in purgatory have something approved and already with "Christ" so that they have something within which experiences an element of that glory even as they are being tried, as we saw in GL1, 682. Thus, the one who is lost has nothing on "the side of heaven" making the experience substantially different from the one in

The question before us is how Balthasar could, at once, deny some intermediary time between our death and resurrection and yet accept purgatory as a kind of intermediary state (without calling it such). The answer is found in the way Balthasar understood the judgment: it did not exist in historical time, nor in supra-heavenly time (eternity), but as some sort of state in between all of them, which has subjective elements connected to time (duration) and yet is not temporal. Balthasar pointed to the then Cardinal Ratzinger's *Eschatology* to make this point:[80]

> Man does not have to strip away his temporality in order to thereby become "eternal"; Christ as judge is *ho eschatos*, the Final One, in relation to whom we undergo judgment *both* after death *and* on the Last Day. In the perspective we have offered here, those two judgments are indistinguishable. A person's entry into the realm of manifest reality is an entry into his definitive destiny and thus an immersion in eschatological fire. This transforming "moment" of this encounter cannot be quantified by the measurements of earthly time. It is, indeed, not eternal but a transition, and yet trying to qualify it as of "short" or "long" duration on the basis of temporal measurements derived from physics would be naïve and unproductive.[81]

The judgment is to be found, not in time (though it affects time), but at the edge of eternity—that is, outside of time and not yet in eternity.[82] Balthasar saw death as an entry into "nontime." While there is a sense of duration subjectively experienced in it, death is a sphere all of its own, without all the qualifications necessary to be called temporal. Holy Saturday, with its silence about Christ, shows us the mystery of death. The date of Holy Saturday took place in history, but the experience of Christ was the experience of the dead with their nontime: "But there exists, on Holy Saturday, the descent of the dead Jesus into hell; that is (speaking very simplistically), his solidarity in nontime with those who have been lost to God."[83]

---

purgatory, even if the source and cause of the suffering is one and the same (because the one in purgatory will have something within them already on the side of glory, that which is already in grace, changing the whole experience of the judgment itself).

80. See TD5, 361.

81. Ratzinger, *Eschatology*, 230. I have extended what Balthasar quotes, to give more context to Ratzinger's thought, so that we can also see that Ratzinger here followed Balthasar in showing the two judgments are related and "indistinguishable."

82. See ET4, 445–46.

83. Ibid., 422.

Historical time is finite, and a person's experience of it ends with death. Balthasar believed that such finality allowed everyone to construct for themselves a complete, composite, integral persona which is revealed only at death, just like the character of a piece of music can only be understood holistically once its end has been played.[84] Death takes the dead out of time, out of finite temporality, so that they can be said to be in nontime, which must not be confused with the nontime of eternity, because eternity is the supra-time of heaven.[85]In other words, when someone dies, they have a non-temporal encounter with Christ, who in his death, entered the non-temporality of death.

Since the judgment exists in its own setting, it can be seen, conventionally, as a transitional state, an intermediary state between death and the resurrection. Since it exists outside of time, there is no time "before" the resurrection (even if, in another sense, the judgment has its own "temporal" quality and "duration" associated with it).[86] In this fashion, Balthasar can be said to agree in spirit, if not with the letter, with the ITC on the intermediate state. Both Balthasar and the ITC believed that something happens between death and the resurrection which allows for our purification. Balthasar said that this "something" was the same thing as the judgment of Christ. But there is a problem: Balthasar claimed that the resurrection and the universal judgment come together, and that they occur only after being purified after purgatory. If this is so, what about the lost? Does not Christian tradition also suggest that they too shall experience a resurrection in their bodies, where they shall then be resurrected for a final and ultimate condemnation?[87] If the wicked, the damned, are to have bodies, how are they to get them following Balthasar's rendering of the resurrection? Balthasar does not give us an answer. This could be seen as an indication that not only did Balthasar hope all would be saved, but that he

84. See TD4, 130.

85. There are three forms of non-temporality which Balthasar discussed, each having a different meaning. "So long as the world endures, there remains for us the unresolvable contradiction between the atemporality of the Cross, the different atemporality of hell, and yet the altogether different all-temporality of heaven." TL2, 359. The Cross is atemporal, for while it happened in history, at a particular time in history, its "remains suprahistorical and ever-'now.'" TD4, 67. Death, however, takes the dead outside of history, and not into eternity, so it brings the dead into a non-historical, non-temporal setting, which gives us them a subjective experience with no objectivity to it.

86. See TD5, 366–67 .

87. See, for example, St. Bonaventure, *Breviloquium*, 230, or the decrees of the Fourth Lateran Council [DZ 429].

leaned toward that hope so much that he sometimes could not discuss any other outcome. In this case, all would be resurrected because all would go through the purgatorial judgment and reach its end. On the other hand, what Andrew Hofer said about Balthasar's presentation of the intermediate state, where his language is varied and confusing, seems to be quite accurate here: "For some, myself included, this Balthasarian language at times jeopardizes the intelligibility of Christian doctrine."[88] This should not lead us to question the intuitions behind Balthasar's theology, but rather, it should help us realize it remains as a speculative human construct, with all the defects as well as opportunities for further engagement and development such a construct brings with it.

IN SUMMARY

God has a plan for every person. They are called to act in the theo-drama with Christ. He has the central role in that drama, but everyone else also has a role in that drama, a role which God gives to them, a role which is to be played out in coordination with Christ. Insofar as they welcome that plan and follow it, they open themselves up to God and his grace. If someone would deny it, and try to set themselves apart from it, creating their vision of their apart from the one they are called to play, they create a sinful, egotistical self, which God hates because of that sin. Everyone, as they fail to meet God's plan for them, establishes in part that sinful self, but as much as they have opened up to God and followed his prompting, they have also integrated themselves into the role or mission God intended for them in life.

Everyone who lives will die. In death, everyone leaves temporal existence and comes face to face with Christ in the a-temporal state of death. There, Christ will judge them, showing them what they have made of themselves in time. Then he will give everyone the opportunity to accept his judgment. If they condemn their sins and cast away all that they have done which made them stand in opposition to God, Christ is willing to take their sin upon him, cast it into the abyss, freeing them then to follow him in his resurrection to the supra-temporal glory of heaven. Whether or not a particular person will accept the opportunity given to them will depend upon the character they have established for themselves in time, whether or not they have fundamentally opened themselves to God and his grace.

88. Hofer, "Balthasar's Eschatology on the Intermediate State," 166.

V

Freedom to Establish Ourselves

THE FUNDAMENTAL CHOICE: LOVE OF SELF OR GOD

Balthasar is very clear, Christ will judge everyone based upon how they measure up to the person God meant them to be. How anyone will respond to that judgment, whether or not they will accept and allow Christ to transform us to become the people God wants us to be, depends upon them and what they have established for themselves as their fundamental choice for or against God.[1]

Our actions in the world allow us to determine who we want ourselves to be, and each action develops the image of the self we create for ourselves, the image which will be judged by Christ. Everything we do serves the affirmation or denial of God, and so anything we do, following the direction of our mind, acts as either an affirmation or a denial of the person God intended us to be. Thus, Balthasar established this as a basic foundation for understanding being in the world:

> First, the world as it concretely exists is one that is always related either positively or negatively to the God of grace and supernatural

1. Pope John Paul II looked at the notion of the fundamental choice, and agreed, in part, with it, as long as it was understood as a deliberate choice for or against God, for or against grace, and not as some existential choice where one's moral actions were seen as disconnected from that fundamental choice for or against God. See Pope John Paul II, *Veritatis Splendor*, sec. 65–68.

> revelation. There are no neutral points or surfaces in this relationship. The world, considered as an object of knowledge, is always already embedded in this supernatural sphere, and in the same way man's cognitive powers operate either under the sign of positive faith or under the negative sign of unbelief.[2]

When we act, we either serve God or the self. We either accept God and what God would have of us, or we close ourselves to God and promote ourselves with egotistical pride. If we reject God, it is because we want to define ourselves, with the limits contained in such self-definition, while an affirmation of God entails an over-coming of such selfishness and seeks God in love, allowing the beloved, God, to define us for ourselves. The norm, the fundamental choice, is either a choice for or against love: "But, in the final analysis, this norm can only be either egoism or love. All other norms are provisional and take their bearings from this ultimate option."[3]

CREATURELY FREEDOM ESTABLISHED IN DIVINE FREEDOM

The infinite capacity of divine freedom makes room for creaturely freedom, giving creaturely freedom a ground on which it can act. God has made room for us, and, in his gracious love, even allows us to choose to oppose him.[4] God intended us to act with love, to relate to him in love, so that we can be molded by God and become the person God wants us to be. Yet, we can choose to act under the direction of the self, to allow the ego to direct the will, closing ourselves off from the grace of God. Either we open ourselves to God, to grace, so as to let God reveal the truth to us, helping us find the truth of our being, or we pick and choose that truth which we want for ourselves, limiting ourselves and our self-disclosure (and thus, self-definition) in the process:

> Thus, a man may be very prudent in his self-disclosure, yet the ground and norm of his prudence may be to tell the truth only insofar as he gains some advantage from it. Or else, a man may have

2. TL1, 30.

3. Ibid., 122.

4. See TD2, 190. This is accomplished through kenosis. As Balthasar explained, God's self-emptying in Jesus Christ is the foundation by which creation is made and so the foundation for our freedom. See *Cavanaugh, "Balthasar, Globalization, and the Problem of the One and the Many,"* 344.

> made it his rule to grant admission only to truth that he wants to hear, that fits his preconceived ideas and does not disturb his self-complacent serenity. And he may also carry out this selection with great prudence. Both deal freely with the truth, both have a law of selection, a law dictated by prudence. But this law is egoism, which contradicts the law of love.[5]

God's infinite freedom permeates everything; it is always present, making room for the choices of his creation.[6] Every action, even those which oppose God, has this infinite freedom as its base. "Infinite freedom, because it is by nature infinite, simply cannot fail to be present wherever finite freedom is. It operates through the latter yet in a latent manner which allows finite freedom to realize itself as genuine decision (for or against its being-in-God)."[7] God's freedom is all around us, providing us the opportunity needed in order to make decisions and act upon them. Our freedom is given to us by the love of God; he has made room for us, and he wants us to respond to him, to his love, with our love.[8]

What exactly does it mean to have "finite freedom?" As Balthasar understood it, there is something paradoxical with the very notion, because finitude suggests limits, while freedom seems to suggest none.[9] Despite such limitations, God's creatures are free. They have the ability to decide how they want to act; they have self-movement.[10] What they decide to do

5. TL1, 122.

6. Creation must be seen as contingent and a freely made decision on God's part: "Von Balthasar continues to explain that creation derives its existence from the freedom of God, so that the world is thereby not necessary in itself, yet it is justified in its existence as an expression of the love between the Trinitarian Persons." Franks, "Trinitarian *Analogia Entis* in Hans Urs von Balthasar," 542.

7. TD2, 316.

8. Rodney Howsare pointed out that this is a key to Balthasar's understanding of freedom: love is the proper ground of freedom. Freedom always has to be understood as relational, relating to our ground of being and to others. Modernity, in its discussion of free will, has ignored love, and so does not properly understand freedom because of this "forgetfulness of love." See Howsare, *Balthasar,* 104.

9. See TD2, 207.

10. Discussions of freedom often begin with the concept of "self-movement," because, as Aidan Nichols put it, "this is the kind of freedom with which we are familiar." Nichols, *No Bloodless Myth,* 66. We know we exist in a world outside of our creation, with an existence that has been handed to us beyond ourselves; but we also know that, in a given moment, we are called to act, and that activity is a free activity, where we choose what we want to do. In this way, because of the fall, Balthasar understood that indifferent freedom serves as a good starting point for discussions of freedom, not because it was the highest form of freedom, but because it is what most initially understand freedom to be.

in a given situation reveals their character. Their actions demonstrate who they make themselves to be. To act, creatures must open themselves up, take in something outside of themselves as something they want to achieve, and find a way to incorporate it into themselves. Everyone seeks after some good to add to themselves, to make themselves greater:

> Certainly finite freedom, the openness to all being, can only strive for something it perceives as good (having a value)—even if in fact it is evil; but it is equally certain that the knowledge of the good *as good* (*bonum honestum*) removes the element of *interest* from such striving, so that the element of *indifference* —- where the one who strives in the clear light of being has in principle superseded all finite 'oppositions'—*turns out to be a new and deeper indifference in which he is able to let the Good 'be', whether it is a finite or infinite Good, simply for the sake of its goodness,* without trying to gain it for himself.[11]

To be free, a person must open themselves up to that which is outside themselves. All actions show such an opening up of the self, in one form or another, to gain something which is outside of that self. As a person closes themselves off to all that is outside themselves, they limit themselves to that which they already have, and their freedom begins to become more and more limited; freedom is possible only insofar as someone continues to open themselves up to that which is outside of their very self. The more someone opens themselves up to infinite freedom, the freer their will becomes, and the more blessed they will be. Full freedom comes when someone opens up completely through obedience to God's direction. "The human person's freedom is only fully illuminated when it is seen to be bound up with a divine and personal freedom that is at pains to promote man's freedom."[12] The Holy Spirit surrounds everyone with grace, giving them the grace necessary for their freedom to remain, giving them the freedom to choose or deny God, and the more they choose God, the more grace will come, bringing greater and greater freedom to them. "The grace of the Spirit sets man free

11. TD2, 211. Indifferent freedom or love again serve as two modalities of willing. Indifferent freedom, as shown here, can merge with love, so as to become what is shown in Ignatian Indifference: the lover freely allows the beloved to make their choices for them, to be led by the beloved instead of trying to dictate the course of action which should be taken. Thus, Balthasar, in discussing the kind of life Christians should have posits this as the proper Christian mode of willing, where Christians open themselves up to God's guidance. See Balthasar, *The Laity and the Life of the Counsel*, 23–24.

12. TD2, 198.

so that he can freely choose, and 'he becomes all the more free the more the Spirit brings him healing, so that he can abandon himself to the divine and gracious mercy.'"[13] Thus, "the Spirit, with his grace, frees man so that he can grasp his genuine human freedom, which, however, he only attains by consenting to that freedom of the divine love that indwells him."[14]

FINITE FREEDOM CLOSED OFF TO ITSELF

Due to sin, sinners have closed themselves off from God's infinite freedom. They have tried to turn themselves into the absolute. Since they are not absolute, they end up imprisoning themselves within the contours of the potentiality they already have within themselves without any more benefit from grace. As long as they look to their own understanding of truth as the truth instead of letting the truth be revealed to them, they will be closed off from any growth, from overcoming the self and being enriched by the greater freedom being offered to them from the true absolute, God.[15] Closed in upon themselves, they have closed themselves off from love, from that which gives truth its power to transform them and make them great.[16] They will possess at best an imitation of truth, a construction which borrows from the truth, but does not have the power or integrity of truth. "The mouth of falsehood can be dripping with individual truths; it can build up astoundingly, flawlessly coherent systems. But, detached from the fundamental movement of love, even these formally correct propositions serve falsehood, and their 'truth' only helps to multiply it."[17] Truth points to greater truth, while falsehood claims the fullness of truth and pretends there is nothing more, nothing greater than that which it already possesses.[18]

13. TL3, 240, where Balthasar is quoting St. Augustine, Letter 157, as a part of his argument.

14. TL3, 240.

15. The greatness of the truth transcends our ability to comprehend it; as long as we try to make it something under our control, we shall not have it. Love allows us to become possessed by the truth instead of trying to possess it, to be open to its revelations instead of presuming what it can and should show to us. In attaining truth, in attaining God, knowledge, however useful, is secondary to love. See O'Donnell, "Truth as Love," 196.

16. See TL1, 111–12.

17. TL1, 123.

18. See TL1, 39.

"Autonomous freedom, once it has been set forth as absolute, can only understand *itself* as the norm of the good."[19] A sinner seeks to justify themselves by claiming their presentation of the truth, their limited possession of the good, as the good itself. As long as they do this, they are trapped by the power of sin. They will hide themselves from the truth, covering themselves from the dictates of any authority outside of themselves. They create, as it were, a protective barrier from the world, even if, in reality, they cannot escape the onslaught of truth which seeks to move them out of their protective egotistical shell. "In this way, the sinner builds a kind of 'bulwark' against the real truth; he hides behind its illusion, knowing all the while that the truth he has 'wickedly suppressed' (Rom 1:18) will eventually come to lay siege against his citadel."[20]

SELF-MEASUREMENT

Truth is the "measure of being."[21] Subjects are those who can unveil the measure of their own being to themselves. "Insofar as it is unveiled to, and no longer concealed from itself, it is being that is inwardly full of light, has emerged into clarity for itself, and is transparent. In the radiance of this light, the subject is able to measure itself, to take its own measure."[22] Self-measurement, however, implies that subjects are trying to understand themselves, to unveil themselves to themselves as it were.[23] The greater they come to know themselves, the greater they can reveal their inner being found within themselves, they more they truly become the people they were meant to be.[24]

In self-unveiling a subject is expected to act under the guidance of love; they open themselves, not only to reveal themselves to others, but to accept the revelation of others, objects of their experience, into themselves.

19. TD4, 163.

20. Ibid., 167.

21. TL1, 75.

22. Ibid., 43.

23. Ferdinand Ulrich, an influence on Balthasar here, suggested that a person can be seen as "an other" to his or her self, so that in order for someone to know themselves, they have to receive themselves with themselves. The self is a gift given by God, and has to be openly accepted by the self for its full realization. See Oster, "The Other and the Fruitfulness of Personal Acting," 194.

24. See Nichols, "The Theo-Logic," 161.

"In themselves, subject and object each have the freedom as to how much they choose to disclose or hide, both in their self-communication to each other and in their willingness to accept the reliability of the truth they have received. "[25] Subjects open themselves up to each other, and in the reception of another into themselves, they come to know and understand themselves: opening up to others is a part of the process of self-revelation.[26] "One's consciousness, one's self-possession and possession of being, can grow only and precisely to the extent that one breaks out of being in and for oneself in the act of communication, in exchange, and in human cosmic *sympatheia*."[27] In this way, in opening themselves up to the world, a subject lets the world and all those within it to reveal themselves to the subject, so that in a loving movement, the subject moves beyond its current position and becomes something greater. It is important, moreover, for them to open themselves up to God, the ultimate Subject, to say yes to what God reveals to them, so that they can accomplish what God intended of them, that is, their personal mission.[28]

Thus, everyone finds themselves to be acting subjects in the world. What they reveal to others through such free activity is their self-testimony.[29] Balthasar believed that truth is manifested in this fashion:

> On the human level, truth is permanently dependent on the free, mutual revelation of human beings who bear witness to each other concerning the truth. Because truth does not lie open before us naturally, it has to be disclosed spiritually. And because this truth, as the truth of a subject, is not subject to verification, the revealing

25. Wigley, *Balthasar's Trilogy*, 126.

That is, we must understand that others, outside of ourselves, are subjects in their own right, revealing themselves to us as objects of our knowledge. With love, we accept them as they reveal themselves to be; we do not try to force or impose upon them constrictions based upon our own objective desires for them. We open up, let their revelation in to us, and allow ourselves to be enhanced by their revelation, and in doing so, we reveal ourselves to them, and enhance them in the same fashion.

26. Balthasar's favorite representation of this lies with that of the child coming to self-understanding through their mother's smile. The infant, in seeing the smile, knows their mother as another, another consciousness, engaging them, so as to understand that there is an I, their own self, coming to and experiencing that other. See Oster, "The Other and the Fruitfulness of Personal Acting," 303–4.

27. LA, 144.

28. See TL1, 80.

29. See Nichols, *Say It Is Pentecost*, 25.

> subject must answer for the truth of his testimony with his full responsibility.[30]

Everyone is responsible for what they do as they reveal themselves to each other. Their actions reveal, more than with words, what they hold dear. "The subject's life thus becomes the proof of its assertion. Life shows what weight its truth actually had. And in fact the truth that it has pronounced comes to the perfection of truth only through this testimony of life."[31]

Everyone can try to hide who they are from the world, to close themselves off from it, to not let anything in from the world to themselves, but if they do so, they will close themselves off from the reception of the graces being offered to them. Yet even in this closure, in this attempt to hide themselves from the world, they reveal something of themselves, showing that, in every moment, they cannot but unveil something of themselves, even if it is our stubborn desire to hide themselves from the world. Everyone is set in motion and must participate as such in a world of motion. "It [a spiritual subject] is forced to its own freedom, in the sense that it is always already set in motion toward this freedom by nature."[32]

There are two-sides to our being. We have an inner, essential nature, and we have that testimony, that public revelation which we unveil what is hidden within. Our inner nature is greater than the phenomenal form in which that unveiling occurs, and yet that form truly represents our inner nature, us, according to way we want to be.[33] "Every entity that has being-for-itself possesses an inside and outside, an intimate and a public sphere. The intimate dimension of beings can appear in a great variety of forms and on a great variety of levels. It increases as things move up the scale of being-for-itself; it reaches its complete form on the level of self-conscious spirit."[34] The form we produce for ourselves is always based upon our inner essence, even if we present ourselves in a way to hide that essence from ourselves through self-deception.[35]

30. TL1, 121.

31. Ibid., 177.

32. Ibid., 80.

33. This relates to Balthasar's notions of form and splendor, where the splendor of a form is the depth of the form, drawing us into the form itself through its luminous, beautiful quality. See Scola, *Hans Urs von Balthasar,* 1–2, and GL1, 118–19.

34. TL1, 82.

35. Humility is required so as not to be self-deceived. Love, being the foundation by which we open ourselves up, allows us to be receptive of the gift of the self given to us, so as to let it be revealed and followed. See Balthasar, *You Have Words of Eternal Life,* 38–40.

The greatest freedom lies in receptivity, of being open to the unveiling of our inner nature, without any attempt to hinder the activity our inner, given nature, would direct us to do. "The highest, freest acts of its spiritual existence are predisposed in its nature."[36] We are given spiritual being from God, and we are called to manifest that being in the world, to unveil it, so as to reveal ourselves, and to identify ourselves with the person God intended us to be. We have our finite freedom because God has called us to act, and he lets us freely decide to act upon the calling he has for us.[37] If we want to experience true freedom, we must be receptive of that persona God has given us and, in loving obedience, reveal it to the world by following the specific mission God has intended for us.[38] Yet, the freedom we have been given allows us to do otherwise, to close ourselves from that mission, to close ourselves from freedom in love, so as to make ourselves something far less than the potential God intended us to actualize.

IN SUMMARY

Freedom is a gift given to everyone by God. A subject does not possess in itself an absolute, infinite freedom, but it is true freedom because the subject has the chance to determine who and what it is to be through its activity. The more it acts, the more it reveals to itself and to others who or what it is. The more a subject acts, the more it can take something from outside itself and incorporate it within, showing in such activity not only its finitude, but its ability to grow and to find its freedom growing as well; on the other hand, if it closes itself off from others, if it tries to limit itself and its activity to the potential already within, it will slowly lose its ability to be free and will be bound to what it already has in itself. In this fashion a subject can either open itself up to God and incorporate grace into it and become great thanks to God, or it can close itself off to freedom and become imprisoned in the self of their own creation. This is, then, the foundation by which a subject determines who and what it is in relation to God, whether or not it will say yes or no to God.

36. TL1, 80.

37. See Oullet, "Paradox and/or Supernatural Existential," 268.

38. See O'Donnell, "Hans Urs von Balthasar," 219–20.

VI

Perdition

RECAPITULATION

Balthasar believed that everyone was made with a specific purpose, a specific mission in the world. This mission is given to them by God, and it defines who they are meant to be as a person. They are given freedom in the exercise (or non-exercise) of that mission. What they have been given is a limited but true freedom. It is finite. Freedom comes to them from an external source, from the external, infinite freedom of God which meets them both externally, in the structures infinite freedom put in place for us to act, as well as internally, in the impulse put in their nature which motivates them to act.[1]

Without grace, without cooperating with Christ, everyone will be unable to achieve their mission in the world. Their mission is tied to Christ, to some aspect of his work in the theo-drama. To achieve their potential, their personhood, everyone is called to unite themselves to Christ and his universal mission. Indeed, when they act with Christ, they are sharing in his universal activity.[2]

1. There is, to be sure, a threat that those structures can be seen as getting in the way of our freedom if they are given too much emphasis. See Quash, "Ignatian Dramatics," 85.

2. See Ackerman, "The Church as Person," 242.

In the incarnation, Christ was able to take on our sins, and take them to the depths of the abyss. He encountered everyone in and through his descent. No one, not even the damned, will be left alone. In this descent, the Son has created a vast distance between himself and the Father, a distance which makes room for everyone in creation. It is in that space which he established where the dead finds themselves meeting the Son. For as they are separated from God, so the Son has separated himself from the Father and meets them in solidarity with them in their separation from God.[3]

Objectively, in his death and resurrection, Christ has brought salvation to humanity, allowing everyone to overcome the imprisonment of sin: "the Son of God snatches us out of the slavery of sin, of the lack of love, of egoism, in order to bring us back from this slavery and self-alienation both to God and to our own selves."[4] Subjectively, it is possible for someone to resist the work of Christ. When someone dies, they will encounter Christ. He will come to them in judgment, showing them what they have made of themselves, what they should have been, and he will give them the opportunity to accept his saving work for them and to be objectively transformed into the person God wants them to be.

FREE TO DENY GOD

Christ's work in the world has given his creatures a new freedom. Christ has given them the chance to turn away from themselves, to deny what they have established for themselves apart from him, and to enter into his life with all the beatitude that he brings to them. He provides the light of grace which makes this possible. Yet, this opportunity has created a new situation, because now his creatures can deny his grace, and give to him a greater denial than they were able to do before. Balthasar declared that decisive rejection of God can only be had in the light of Christ, for it is only after Christ that a no to God is allowed to intensify to its maximum limit.[5] The more love God manifests to his creatures, the more they can act in resistance to that love.[6] Nihilistic atheism only emerges after the incarnation,

3. See Power, "The Holy Saturday Experience," 35.
4. GL7, 408.
5. See TD5, 22.
6. See Nichols, *No Bloodless Myth,* 189.

because it is only after God has fully revealed himself in Christ can God be properly denied.[7]

In effect, because of Christ's accomplishments, his creatures are now offered two choices. They can continue to follow the lines of self-determination in rejection of the person God intended them to be, or they can open themselves up to God, through love, so as to become the person God wants them to be:

> Now the herald's cry that proclaims the gospel the call to decision is clear: it demands that a choice be made between two freedoms — a freedom, which may take a personal or collective form, of innerwordly self-determination (αὐτάρκεια), and a freedom of self-giving in faith's obedience to the love of God. The one who chooses self-determination will remain in the 'servitude' of the world and will be alienated from God, while the one who chooses self-giving has his home with God and is a 'pilgrim and stranger' (1 Pete 1.1; 2.11; Heb 11.13) and a 'resident alien' (1 Pet 1.17; cf. Heb 11.9) in this world.[8]

Because of Christ's accomplishments, there emerges the possibility that someone could choose absolute self-determination, to close themselves off from God's will and to choose complete, unending alienation from God. This is how eternal perdition reveals itself in Balthasar's theology. The lost one will say to Christ, "I do not want to become the person you would have me to be, but to remains as I am, in this state I have made for myself."

THE RESURRECTION ESTABLISHED THE POSSIBILITY OF PERDITION

According to Balthasar, Jesus renders judgment upon the dead until they accept the person God intends them to be. They must allow Christ to transform them, to make of them as he will. In this sense, judgment is an act of love, for as it reveals to each person what God wants of them, it is also offers them the ability to accept the grace which can then transform them to become the person God wants them to be.[9] Everyone will be given the opportunity to open themselves completely to grace, to become full of grace, so that it perfects them and elevates them to the beatific state. If they deny

7. See LA, 91–92.

8. GL7, 501.

9. See Balthasar, *Does Jesus Know Us*, 83.

that grace, all they have in their encounter with Christ will be his judgment. In this fashion, for those who will be saved, Christ's judgment becomes the source of purgatorial grace, but for those who reject such grace, it establishes them in their hell. God created his creatures to participate in the divine life, but if they reject it, they lose everything.

Hell, eternal perdition, is possible only after the resurrection of Christ, for it is by his entrance into the realm of the dead, his experience of its fullness, and his transcendence of it by the resurrection, he has the ability to judge sin from within and to declare its proper end:

> In the rising from the dead, Christ leaves behind him Hades, that is the state in which humanity is cut off from access to God. But, by virtue of his deepest Trinitarian experience, he takes 'Hell' with him, as the expression of his power to dispose, as judge, the everlasting salvation or the everlasting loss of man.[10]

Christ has opened up a place in God where the judgment of creation can take place.

OBJECTIFICATION AND DEPERSONALIZATION OF THE DAMNED

Does this suggest creatures are mere objects for God? As much as they are sinners who have not become true, authentic persons in Christ, Balthasar's theological anthropology would suggest the answer is yes. Sin is objectified in Christ, and to refuse to have that sin removed from them objectifies them as well, for it is only in releasing their self-made image to become the person God meant them to be that they find freedom and become a true subject. The images of who they think they should be, the reified individual they have become due to sin, is meant to be cast off, turned into an effigy which is put to the fire of judgment.[11] What saints saw when they experi-

10. MP, 177. According to Edward T. Oakes, this differentiation between "the abode of the dead" before Christ and "hell" or "eternal perdition" finds itself set up in the theological tradition by Augustine. See Oakes, "'He Descended into Hell,'" 227.

11. Balthasar shared this idea with Adrienne von Speyr. See O'Donnell, "Truth as Love," 199–200. Interestingly enough, he saw this as the truth behind Luther's idea of *simul justus et peccator*, not that the one who is saved will have any sin, but that for all who are saved, there is something in them which is also damned. "There is a certain convergence of the two views, insofar as no one who knows he has an effigy in hell can 'any longer consider himself righteous': 'this temptation is passed; he knows he is a saved person: Hell holds his copy': '*simul damnatus et redemptus*.'" TL2, 357.

enced hell, or what is expressed in Dante's journey into hell in the *Divine Comedy*, are the effigies of sinners, images which represent them but are not necessarily the sinners themselves.[12]

All sinners have such effigies made from their sins. Christ makes it so that they can be removed. They must unload these effigies, these figures of sin, upon Christ through confession. Such confession can be accomplished in sacramental confession, but it can also be done through self-judgment in the presence of Christ.[13]

If someone does not turn their sins over to Christ, they become trapped, unchanging, immobile, objectified by them in such a way that there can be no hope for them because there is no possibility for them to change. It is only by opening themselves to the truth that they can grow. Everyone needs to be receptive of the truth, but that openness requires them to remove from themselves anything which stands in the way of such truth, that is, sin.[14] The image they create for ourselves, the image which will be judged, as well as the response they have to the judgment itself (whether or not they will welcome Christ's judgment and so cast off that false), all manifest and reveal what was accomplished in time.

There is a sense of freedom which comes from time. "From moment to moment, presence is always just now coming toward us [*zukommt*]. This is its futurity [*Zukünfigkeit*]. The future is not a state of being or time lying alongside, and separate from the present, but a direction within the present, within existence itself."[15] Every moment a creature experiences this rush of being, and every moment they are given the opportunity to accept it and

12. Balthasar believed the vision of hell in Dante's Inferno was of these effigies, indicating not who was among the damned, but rather the what would be cast aside into hell. See GL3, 99.

13. See TL2, 356. Balthasar pointed out that, after those sins are put into the purifying fire of God, there remains a kind of image, the form of the effigy, which reminds us of the battle against sin we faced in our lives. This goes to show that with Balthasar, there is no concept of a purely empty hell.

Indeed, as Lösel pointed out, "Individual sins do not affect their agent in an accidental way. Rather, they affect the very substance of a person. With every sin the sinner loses a substantial part of him- or her-self, which gets disposed into hell. Thus even justified sinners who enjoy eternal beatitude in heaven have given a part of themselves to hell." Lösel, "A Plain Account of Christian Salvation," 152.

14. One could perhaps call this openness "faith" as Victoria Harrison has done in her reading of Balthasar. This is because someone must have faith that there is something out there to open up to it. See Harrison, "Putman's Realism and Von Balthasar's Religious Epistemology," 70.

15. TL1, 196.

the infinite range of experiences it offers to them.[16] If they do not open themselves up to receive this gift, in each and every moment, what was offered in that moment will then be lost.[17] They need to constantly open themselves to that gift, so that they can take the grace offered by it, with each moment the offer of grace becomes greater and greater, the more such grace is accepted; without such openness, they will become stuck where they are, and indeed, an unwillingness to open up to the present moment and the future which comes from it leads them to become, as it were, stuck in the past. Being is always being presented to us moment to moment; it is in flux, making every moment of being a precious gift, and what is not accepted cannot be brought back.[18] The past has passed away, and the present contains the seeds of its own demise, that is, it will move on and become a part of the past, which Balthasar explained, is "precisely what gives every moment of existence its infinite, eternal weight."[19]

What a person has not opened up to and received in a given moment will not come back to them; they must keep themselves open and accept the graces given to them as the future comes to them, the ever infinite richness and variety of being that emerges from that future. Because the future comes to them from the present moment, what they have closed off in the moment will determine what the future, with its variety of graces, can offer to the person. For someone to cut themselves off from the transformation and graces coming to them from the moment, they end up "living," as it were, only in the past, and the more they do this, the more they limit themselves, until at last, there is no exit, no chance of transformation, no chance of change. Beatitude takes all the glory of the rush of being coming from the future, while perdition finds itself closed off from that grace by its attachment to the past. "Eternal life is a life whose present contains an eternal future, but no past. Eternal damnation, on the other hand, would

16. What is being offered from moment to moment is more than a person can take in for themselves; that is, each moment of time, with the gift being offered, the creature has a flexibility as to what gifts, what graces, they take in to themselves. See TL1, 197.

Thus, the future comes out of the present, out of the infinite gift which is not overcome by what is taken in by the present. For each moment, there is the recognition that whatever good is accepted graciously by the creature, there is still more to come due to the infinite capacity of the gift of time presented to each and every creature in each moment of existence. See Schindler, *Hans Urs von Balthasar and the Dramatic Structure of Truth*, 85–86.

17. See TL1, 197.

18. Ibid., 198.

19. Ibid.

be a life whose present is turned entirely toward the past. It would thus be pure hopelessness."[20] If someone closes themselves off from grace, they cut themselves off from the loving activity which allows them to make room for being, and so they become stuck, incapable of any further movement. In this fashion Balthasar explained that, "eternal damnation would be the total evacuation of this every greater plentitude from existence. It would be the futility and absurdity of becoming a state."[21]

In this way, Balthasar suggested that hell is a kind of timelessness, as pure objectivity, as imprisonment, completely opposite of the subjectivity and freedom of heaven.[22] Balthasar pointed out that although we conventionally say hell is eternal, this often causes confusion, because we mistake this as the same kind of eternity associated with heaven.[23] For this reason, he suggested that while the term "eternal" is used for hell, hell is better understood as "un-ending," for the one who suffers hell is trapped as in a kind of stasis of their own making, the stasis of perpetual judgment. Thus, when talking about various experiences of hell, Balthasar wrote:

> They are, after all, characterized by a total withdrawl of any temporal dimension, by being tightly bound into the most constricted, airless and exitless now and this is the vilest of all locations ("under Lucifer's tail," as Mechtilde of Magdeburg writes once), which, in theological terms, implies the restrictedness of the mortal egotist, who has rejected every form of love and is thus thrown back upon his own simultaneously affirmed and detested I (A=A).[24]

"Eternal" or unending perdition is had when one finds themselves trapped in that self, "shriveling into a disconsolate immovable now."[25] That self cannot be said to be truly a person—indeed, it is better to describe is as an unperson, because it has not taken on the qualities God has intended.[26] Evil takes persons and makes them impersonal. This is why Balthasar, when he discussed demonic powers, he referred to them as impersonal forces, for they have lost whatever personality they might have had in their rebellion

20. Ibid., 198.

21. Ibid., 199.

22. Hell loses all the positive qualities of being, as it is closed off and becomes, as it were, timeless existence.

23. See DWH, 125.

24. Ibid., 129.

25. Ibid., 133.

26. See Nichols, *No Bloodless Myth*, 130–31.

against God.[27] They are forces, yes, but they have become forces outside of any sense of self-will, because to be a person is to be free, while those who have lost their personhood therefore have lost their freedom.[28]

THE FREEDOM TO DENY FREEDOM: THE INTERNAL CONTRADICTION OF HELL

The devil can no longer be seen as a person but as an impersonal power; other creatures can follow his example and depersonalize themselves. If love is the basis of grace, then its rejection is hate, and it is why the devil himself is said to be full of hate.[29] Of course this depersonalization must result from a choice from someone who, at one time, had free will. It is the choice to deny God, to deny being, to deny freedom which comes from accepting being, and so the choice to deny the personification God hopes for them. Slowly in their denial of God, in their sin, they establish a habit which they do not overcome, which is the foundation of their depersonalization: "It is possible for him to become so hardened in his freedom that he must pursue to the end the path he has chosen in opposition to God."[30] Thus, they can harden their heart so much that we will always say no to God. This is what is needed for perdition. They must utterly repudiate the grace being offered to them by God by turning inward away from God and establishing a habitual activity which will all them to continuously deny the grace of God.[31]

This hardening of the heart is the attempt of created freedom to identify itself as absolute, to try to claim for itself infinite freedom by and in itself.[32] Despite how they would like to be absolute, they will know that they

27. See DWH, 145–46.

28. In his reading of Irenaeus, Balthasar saw this point being made in relation to humanity possessing the image of God: that image given to them represents the persons God intended them to be, but they are still free to accept or deny that image, that is, free to accept or deny that intention of God. With original sin, that image became disfigured, limiting the freedom of the human creature, but in perdition, that image is lost, and with it, the person's freedom. See GL2, 75.

29 See TD5, 203.

30. Ibid., 288.

31. Ibid., 298.

32. This thought, that an individual closes in on themselves and it is this self-closure which creates the condition of hell, is common in many modern religious thinkers. Balthasar shared it with Bulgakov. See Martin, *Hans Urs von Balthasar And the Critical Appropriation of Russian Religious Thought,* 138.

are not; they will know that there is an infinite freedom outside of themselves, a freedom which they have denied for themselves. The more they deny themselves from this participation in infinite freedom, the more they enclose themselves in the trap they set for themselves by themselves, until at last, they have entirely closed themselves off to infinite freedom and end up suffering the pains of hell. There is a contradiction involved, because even their finite freedom still comes from and is bound by the infinite freedom which is denied, but this knowledge itself helps establish the suffering of hell. There can be no peace in a creature which seeks to be its own origin and foundation, which is what claims of self-absoluteness would be, knowing it cannot be either.[33]

THE CONSUMING FIRE

Christ took sin upon himself, and through that act, he experienced the objectiveness of sin in his own experience as one of the dead. This meant that he subjectively experienced, in solidarity with the dead, the sense of abandonment from God that sin brings to us.[34] By taking on sin, he was able to establish a place for it and its objectivity in his creation. Hell is that place where all the sin which Christ leaves behind after his resurrection from the dead is said to reside. What is left there is what is condemned by Christ. That is, what we will find in hell is either that sin which has been removed from the sinner, or the sinner themselves, objectified by the sin which they did not abandon.[35] Those who have hardened their hearts and rejected God do so by their own initiative. God entices everyone to come to him; but it must be a free choice; sinners must make the choice to open themselves up from their shell of the self and follow Christ.[36] What is done in life will be judged in death, but in that judgment what will be made clear is whether or not someone in their actions, in their life, have made a fundamental choice for or against God. Until the judgment, it might appear someone has accepted or denied God, but it is only after their presentation of themselves by Christ, and the comparison of it to what God intended them to be, will someone know their true reaction to God, and if theyo-

33. See TD5, 307.

34. See Gonzalez, "Hans Urs von Balthasar and Contemporary Feminist Theology," 587–88.

35. See TD5, 314. See also, Sara, "Descensus ad Inferos," 553.

36. TL2, 75.

pened up and accepted the full transformation to the person God intended them to be or not.[37]

At the core, our actions indicate choices either to open ourselves up to the fullness of being or to close ourselves off from it and so attach ourselves to non-being. "Authentic choice always intends the whole: being or nonbeing."[38] Thus, the eschatological decision for or against God, made in the judgment but resting upon the fundamental choice established during life, reveals whether someone stands with God and being or against God with non-being. The greatest choice we have can be said to be either for negation of the self we made for ourselves, negated through love, or for the negation of love for the promotion of that falsely established and highly individualized self. A person can only exist in loving relation to others, and so to be a person is to love, while to deny love is to deny personhood for oneself. The Christian faith on the Trinity establishes this point by pointing out how the persons of the Trinity are in loving relationship with each other, and not closed off individuals. Each particular person in the Trinity finds its understanding of its own personal "I" is found in relation to the other persons, and not cut off and individualized in and of itself: "The Christian view sees the individual I as an *imago Trinitatis* in which each hypostasis exists solely for the sake of the others and can only understand itself in that context."[39]

When confronted by Christ in their particular judgment, the decisions they have made for themselves in relation to the fundamental option becomes clear. The judgment will be harsh. For the love of God puts to flame all that is unworthy, all that is unredeemable: it is wrathful even as it can prepare someone for salvation. What is said universally about the world in the coming of God in the Apocalypse is also true for the soul who is judged: the fire of God seeks to heal, but it devours that which has not been not turned over to him:

> This drama, in which God's absoluteness (understood as power or as love) touches the sphere of the fragile creature, can only be

37. This, once again, is why Balthasar said no one should not assume the outcome of the judgment. Self-deception could cause someone to justify their closure to God by making an appearance of holiness, while someone who is struggling to open up to God, might have a difficult time doing so during their life, and so find their struggle affirmed by the grace given to them in the judgment and what they truly desired will be given to them. See DWH, 85.

38. TL2, 30.

39. TL3, 264.

> a fiery event, a history of fire, made up either of devouring or of healing flames; and everyone who looks back from the vantage of the Apocalypse, having heard the account of the entire action, is bound to sense this, in some fashion at least.[40]

Balthasar found much value in these words of Paul: "each man's work will become manifest; for the Day will disclose it, because it will be revealed with fire, and the fire will test what sort of work each one has done. If the work which any man has built on the foundation survives, he will receive a reward. If any man's work is burned up, he will suffer loss, though he himself will be saved, but only as through fire" (1 Cor 3:13–15 RSV). This fire heals sinners by removing from them the false constructed image of the self they have established in and through their sins; anything which they have done in opposition or contradiction to God and his grace is thrust into the fire to be consumed.[41] That is, anything which they have done in rejection of love, and therefore, for themselves apart from love, will be removed, and in the process, they will see and learn how to become more and more of the person God intended them to be, and so they will see beyond themselves and enter into greater and greater communion with God and others. It destroys their egotistical shell, leaving them to understand their new personal self is relational, discovered in awe: "The fire destroys all this 'I'-talk and trains one in saying 'you' and 'we.'"[42]

It is God's love which acts upon the soul, seeking its transformation in the fiery judgment. It is God's love which bring someone to their judgment, and therefore, into the crisis which leads them to find themselves either stuck in perdition or freed from sin and granted salvation. It is because Christ comes to everyone in love that even if the judgment is something to fear, there is hope to be had in it. It is what allows them to be saved. It is the means by which all the bad choices and decisions which they have done are able to be removed from them so that they can find their proper place with God. His gracious love changes them, if they have opened themselves to it and accepted it. "This love penetrates and purifies the soul. Its effect is

40. TD4, 59.

41. Balthasar suggests that the egotistical self, all that is made in and through an egotistical isolation, is the "wood" which burns in the purifying fire: "The work made out of wood is a work done to honor one's own ego; this work must be dismantled down to its foundations, stripped for its own good of its works, has to learn from the ground up of this holy poverty in spirit." ET4, 455.

42. ET4, 455.

like that of fire on wood."[43] Just as wood is changed by fire, so they become something different from the fiery love of God. Their response to God's love must be selfless love. To be saved, they need to love, which means, they must overcome all forms of egoism and surrender themselves to God. Balthasar was able to express this point through his examination of the theological significance of St. John of the Cross, because John of the Cross was able to explore the purgation which frees someone from sin and transforms them to a lover of God:

> But if she is to do this, the soul is required to come out from the confines of life, and such emergence is possible only through a love stronger than Hell, a life stronger than death. This love does not attain the beloved by its own powers, but jumps and is caught by the open arms of the love of God, who transforms the soul from being a lover into a beloved.[44]

Obviously, for the one who continues to reject God, this fiery love of God does not transform them, even though God wants to do so. This creates unending torment for them. God's love brings about the sufferings of hell, not because it seeks to create such suffering, but because it seeks to transform them and will work to transform them until that transformation has taken effect. Perdition knows no such transformation. The individual willfully cuts themselves off from grace, from all that would allow such transformation to take effect, so that they will find their individual existence shrinking as they experience this judgment, and for them it will be experienced as the never-ending wrath of God. As this takes place in a transitory, non-temporal state, perdition itself is found in this non-temporal, non-eternal state, which is not open to eternity.[45] The declaration that hell is a state or inner condition is, as Balthasar noted in *Mysterium Paschale,* an idea which was not unique to him, but found throughout Christian history:

> It may be useful to recall by way of preamble that, for one entire Christian line of tradition, 'Hell' has been conceived primarily as an inner condition (and not as a 'place' or an 'exterior ordeal'). Beginning with Augustine, this tendency continues, via, for example, Honorius of Autun and Dietrich of Freiberg, not to speak of Scotus Eriugena or Nicholas of Cusa. To this there corresponds

43. GL3, 111.

44. Ibid., 119.

45. See Martin, *Hans Urs von Balthasar and the Critical Appropriation of Russian Religious Thought,* 143.

> to the notion that, in Hell, a particular experience of time reigns, that of a *tempus informe:* a bringing to a standstill of the runaway course of time (and so a paradoxical pendant to the structure of eternity in the sense of life everlasting).[46]

The "*tempus informe*" of hell is the establishment of the constant experience of the self-enclosed I of the damned. Their state of being is not temporal, but they experience that state as their new experience of existence, of being stuck in a moment of existence as the new meaning of time for the damned: "Hell will be regarded increasingly as the condition of the self-enclosed 'I,' the 'I' unliberated by God, to the point of becoming a constitutive dimension, no less, of present existence."[47]

Once again, hell is shown to be a state of existence which is cut off from change, cut off from freedom; those stuck there have chosen the self they have created for themselves instead of turning themselves over to God, and so do not have the freedom and liberation which God's grace brings to them. The fiery judgment of Christ, since it comes to us with the loving grace of God, gives the one being judged the ability to put off that self, to transfer it to Christ, so to let it be condemned by not only Christ, but themselves as well; they must cooperate with God, overcome that false, selfish core, in order to allow the healing grace of God come in and perfect them. Balthasar indicated everyone undergoes judgment. For those who are saved, it comes to an end when the sinner accepts the fullness of the judgment and agrees with it; this is done when the sinner entirely puts themselves over to Christ and sees him and all things in him and not in their falsely created notions established by their false construction of the self. They will, moreover, agree with the judgment that they will paradoxically wish to stay in judgment and its suffering for as long as any sin causes pain to the God-man. "The purification (So it has been said) then comes to an end when the one whose eyes are transfixed on the One pierced for our sins would be ready to *stay* in the fire for as long as sin (not mine but any sin) is still causing pain in the God-man."[48] This transformation shows how they have become changed and imitate God in being persons who exist in love, and this is what qualifies them to be saved.

46. MP, 76–77.

47. Ibid., 77.

48. ET4, 456.

THE SELF-MADE HELL

By overcoming the self which they have created for themselves through their use of their limited freedom, a sinner can integrate themselves into the freedom of God and become truly free. Everyone has been created by grace to be a person in Christ, realizing their freedom in a mission established for them by God. Insofar as someone has failed to do this, they are a sinner, but grace remains available, thanks to Christ, allowing those who have fallen into sin to overcome their sin, to overcome its imposition upon their persona, and so that they once again can become the person God intended for them. Such limited freedom can be used so as to constantly deny all such grace, to close themselves off from God and God's intentions for them. Each and every no to God, each and every no to his offer of grace, establishes greater and greater limits of freedom and being upon the one who denies God. The absolute and continuous denial of God becomes then the limit of the individual's existence, and that existence then is their own self-made hell. While they have achieved their will, they have attained themselves and only themselves, they still find themselves unsatisfied; it is, as Aidan Nichols suggests, a hunger which remains with them, because though they got what they willed, they find their will is unable to satisfy their desires.[49]

This reveals that eternal perdition, hell, is inherently contradictory by nature. The sinner who wills for it gets what they desire, but they do not desire what they will get. They are caught up in themselves, and they hate what they have made for themselves. They continue to exist in this state of being, and yet the negativity which led them to hell shows that they are engaging non-being and so hell is in some way the attachment to that which is not. Those in it are constantly perishing, always diminishing, but never annihilated. Quoting and adding to his thought the words of Adrienne von Speyr and her own experiences of hell, Balthasar took this internal contradiction of hell seriously, writing:

> First, there is a contradiction in the essence of hell itself, because insofar as hell is discarded sin, hell is and at the same time it is not. Consequently, it is ultimately something that is at once atemporal-eternal and self-destroying, perishing, 'dragged down' 'eddying

49. See Nichols, *No Bloodless Myth*, 69.

> down.'" Being both, hell is only "dregs." "Of course that is not possible, . . . and yet it is."[50]

Eternal perdition can only come about through a conscious rejection of grace, that is, through a rejection of divine love.[51] Before the death and resurrection of Christ, death prevailed over humanity, leaving those who died in a rather ambiguous state of existence. The work of Christ involved the transformation of death by taking death upon himself. Christ experienced the hopelessness of the grave in a way far greater than anyone else, which allowed him to offer everyone the chance of grace. He is the authentic judge of the dead.[52]

Only after his resurrection did hell, eternal perdition, become possible; it was only after the resurrection that someone can fully say no to God because the full offer of grace had to be there for it to be rejected. Everyone will encounter Christ and be judged by him according to what they have and have not done. It is at that judgment when they will see the results of God's offers of grace, which, if embraced will make them become the person we are meant to be in God's eyes, and be saved. "The love that God bestows on me makes me become what I truly am, and what I will eventually be. It makes the 'I' become the self, the real person that God wants to see and desires to possess."[53] This requires self-surrender, surrender to God's vision of what God expects someone to be.[54] It is the disintegration of the false I to the realization of the real I God desired for the one being judged.[55] This is what is meant by obedience to God. It is, as Werner Löser stated, "self-abandonment to God's call, in choosing God's choice."[56]

It is possible that someone will hold on to their desire to be themselves, for themselves alone, denying God's call to personhood, and so reject that grace which allows them to become truly free persons in God. This is true and proper disobedience, true and proper denial of God and all that is external to the self and what the self desires to create for itself. If such disobedience becomes someone's final and absolute choice, Balthasar said

50. TL2, 351. Balthasar is quoting Adrienne von Speyr's *Kreuz und Hölle*.

51. See ET4, 434–35.

52 See MP, 176–79.

53. Balthasar, *Engagement with God*, 24.

54. See TD5, 365.

55. See ibid., 366.

56. Löser, "The Ignatian Exercises in the Work of Hans Urs von Balthasar," 107.

they have abandoned all grace and so will have only the perpetual experience of judgment before Christ:

> It arises from the inner reality of the grace flowing from the Cross: once a person has refused to accept the gift of this grace there is nothing left "behind" the Cross but the specter of judgment. For the man "who has spurned the Son of God, and profaned the blood of the covenant by which he was sanctified" "there no longer remains a sacrifice for sins, but a fearful prospect of judgment" (Heb 10:29, 26). Those who do not value the grace of God in Christ "crucify the Son of God on their own account and hold him in contempt." Ground like this, bringing forth only thorns and thistles, "is worthless and near to being cursed; its end is to be burned" (Heb 6:6ff).[57]

In this way, everyone must either give up their attachment to the image and idea of the self they have established for themselves and become truly free in the new persona given to them in and through Christ, or they will cling to that self, to a static, unchanging, determined form of existence, where our their personhood (and freedom) is lost. While conventionally hell is often discussed using terms indicative of time and eternity, in reality, neither term does the experience of hell justice. It is the static closure from time and eternity of the one who rejects eternal, infinite freedom. In a footnote, Balthasar had Adrienne von Speyr explain this:

> In hell, however, time as such is 'lost'; the attempt 'to express it presupposes that one lives under the law of time and not in the timelessness that is neither eternity nor past time; it is not even the moment . . . ; even as time it is nothing; and if time is nothing, it cannot be lost. This is precisely the point: one has lost everything one does not possess. But what is not possessed can also not be lost.[58]

There can be no exit from hell if someone truly has established themselves in it. They have all they have made for themselves. They cannot give themselves the being which is needed for the freedom to exit hell, and they have turned in upon themselves so they reject, in perpetuity, the grace Christ offers them which would give them the freedom to exit hell. They have walled themselves in. While Christ, in his judgment, seeks to bring down that wall of sin and cast it aside in the fire of hell, they avoid him and his work as they

57. Balthasar, *Does Jesus Know Us*, 81.

58. TL2, 349 n. 100.

continue to look inward, always inward, establishing and re-establishing that barrier between Christ and themselves. In this fashion, they can be said to reside in an ever-diminishing but never extinguished existence, experiencing in perpetuity the judgment of Christ as the fires of hell.

IN SUMMARY

Freedom is at the heart of Balthasar's eschatology. Humans are made to be free. God has given everyone the freedom of self-determination. In that freedom, they are called to open themselves to God, receive the grace which he offers them, and to find themselves becoming the person God intended them to be. When they do this, they find their freedom growing as they become a true subject in Christ. Those who deny God, deny grace. They will not become free subjects in Christ, but instead, they will find their very freedom diminishing as their existence becomes less subjective and more objective. It is in death that what one has made of themselves is determined by the judgment of Christ. In that judgment, if someone has chosen to be receptive of grace, Christ will work with them to purify them from all the sins of their life, and bring them around to perfection and lead them to salvation. If they have denied grace, then the judgment will never end. The person will have lost their freedom, lost the ability to open up to grace, and so will be turned inward as Christ seeks to purify them from their sins; they will constantly build up what Christ would tear down, the barrier of sin which angers God, and so their judgment will go on with no end. They will be lost forever.

VII

Summary and Analysis of Balthasar's Eschatology

THE DIFFICULTY WITH BALTHASAR'S THEOLOGY

It can be rather difficult to pin down Balthasar's explanation for perdition. His ideas are dispersed throughout a multitude of his writings. They have to be tracked down and brought together in order to demonstrate that he seriously considered the possibility of hell and accepted its potential as real. His eschatological interest was not in studies of perdition, but in the hope that all might be saved. This explains why there is no major text which succinctly puts all of his ideas on perdition together for the casual reader to read. For this reason, it was necessary to take Balthasar at his word, and explore what he said on the possibility of perdition, to see that he indeed takes it as a real possibility and that he explored, in part, how that possibility could be explained.

Balthasar believed that God desired that all should be saved. This, he believed, should be seen in our desire for others, that we also should desire and hope that all would be saved. Nonetheless, God gave his creatures free will. Except for the saints, there is no way to know how any particular person has acted in relation to God, whether or not they have accepted his offer of grace or utterly denied it. This is why Balthasar consistently said that he did not know whether or not everyone would be saved.[1] In dealing with perdition, as with eschatology and theology in general, Balthasar understood his conclusions were imprecise. He knew that there would always be more of the truth to encounter than what we, as finite creatures, can bring with us in our theological reasoning, and so to eschatological reflections.[2] His eschatology is founded upon his belief in God's gracious gift of freedom; his hope is that such freedom will be accepted by all, because of the glory and joy involved with it, but he knew that was the extent of what he could say. Some could, for their own reasons, reject that freedom and lose themselves in their objective rejection of grace.

CONCERN ABOUT JUDGMENT

Balthasar's eschatology focuses on the judgment of Christ. All will face him when they die. Justice demands the condemnation of sin. Everyone will come to Christ to have their sin judged and condemned. This makes the judgment something which no one should take lightly. Nonetheless, God is love, and that love is also manifest in the judgment. Because of that love, there is reason for hope that in and through the judgment, a sinner can cast off their sin and truly become the person God intends them to be. Everything, even the judgment, is centered upon love, and the self-emptying, kenotic nature, of love, as love does not hold to itself but willfully gives itself to the beloved. If the sinner has any love for God within, it will allow them to deny themselves, deny their shallow, sinful self, and truly open up to God.[3]

While Christ offers his saving love to those being judged, there remains that judgment. No one should presume they are among the saved, nor that they are among the damned. Until the judgment, until Christ's revelation of who everyone is and how they have accepted or denied the grace given to them in life, the end result of the judgment is not known. In a way, no one truly knows themselves until it is revealed to them by Christ. In life, everyone should strive to love God and accept his grace, but there is the possibility some will fool themselves in thinking what they do is out of

1. See Taylor, "The Hope for Universal Salvation," 43.

2. This is true even for the church and her teachings, which is why theological development is possible. See Balthasar, *A Theology of History*, 108.

3. Love is therefore a kind of self-kenosis for everyone, especially the persons of the Godhead. See Gawronski, *Word and Silence*, 95.

love, when it is not, or out of spite, when it is not, and so the true meaning of their actions will be hidden even from themselves.

LOVE OVERCOMES THE BONDAGE OF SIN

Sin leads us into bondage, and prevents sinners from experiencing the freedom which God desires to give to them. Sin leads to an egotistical, individualistic alienation from the world, and also alienation from oneself. Eternal perdition can be seen as the objectification of a subject, where it no longer is free to move, no longer free to decide; it is stuck as if in a single "infinite" point. Sin reinforces itself by its own logic; though it is rare, Balthasar did discuss the "habit of sin,"[4] and used it as a means to explain the bondage of sin. This is an area which Balthasar could have, and probably should have, developed further; what exactly creates the habit? How does sin become habitual? Once it is habitual, can someone truly "open up" and maneuver out of it? Perhaps, for many, the answer lies with purgatory, but since others seem to be able to overcome bad habits outside of the judgment, perhaps there are other means by which they can be overcome. If those means could be found, perhaps they can help people prepare themselves for the coming judgment of Christ and cast aside more of their sin this side of the judgment than wait and hope they can do so after death.

As long as sinners are attached to their egotistical "self," they are unable to open up to God and to let him reveal to them the person they are meant to be. Detachment, therefore, must be possible, and it is possible through the Holy Spirit. "The grace of the Spirit sets man free so that he can freely choose, and 'he becomes all the more free the more the Spirit brings him healing, so that he can abandon himself to the divine and gracious mercy.'"[5] Such detachment is manifest in love, for love is self-denial.

JUDGMENT AND THE SECOND DEATH

Christ has objectively redeemed all things. Objectified-subjects now stand beneath Christ's throne of judgment and are given a choice: to become free subjects in Christ by pushing off the objective bonds of sin (dying, therefore, to the objectified self), or else, to close off all possibility of being free

4. HW, 9.

5. TL3, 240. Here, Balthasar is quoting St. Augustine, Epist. 157, 8 [221].

subjects, and to further "isolate" themselves, to complete the objectification of themselves, where all subjective freedom is removed. The timeless character of death for the sinner who remains in sin is different from the timeless character of death for the saved who finds their place in eternity. Eternity is unlimited freedom in grace; "eternal death," is the infinite expansion of a "timeless" judgment without end.

Death, moreover, is lonely, because there is no community for us to associate with when we are in the realm of the dead.[6] "Man dies alone. Whereas life always says togetherness—even in the mother's womb—so much so that an individual person can neither come into being alone, nor endure, not even be thought. Death manages to suspend this law of community for an a-temporal moment."[7] While the death mentioned in the passage above is death as it existed before the cross, this also is what happens to the sinner who opposes God to the very end.

For Balthasar, the question is always the question of love. Will someone follow through with the love God has shown to them with love of their own, or will they reject God's love and therefore, reject God? The latter only comes from the sinner who has entirely cut themselves off from love. They become, as it were, pure contention (or hate). With such hate, they completely oppose God by declaring themselves as the absolute. Since their very existence is outside of their control, the contradiction between their assertion of absoluteness with the fact that they cannot be absolute burns them within, and this is a great part of their suffering if they end up among the damned.[8]

THE OPPORTUNITY FOR SALVATION

Jesus, the Second Person of the Trinity, has made a place for everyone, that is, for the whole of creation, to participate in the divine life:

> The world with its freedom finds a resting place in the final plan of God between God the Father and God the Son and is allowed to

6. The then Cardinal Ratzinger indicated how such loneliness of the dead highlights the relationship between death and sin, for sin divides and keeps people apart, makes them without love. The loneliness of death is the manifestation of the unlove which is sin. See Ratzinger, *Introduction to Christianity*, 238–39.

7. Balthasar, *The Moment of Christian Witness*, 30.

8. Thus hell can be said to be a "state" and not really a "place." See Wainwright, "Eschatology," 120.

> participate in that highest freedom which, Christianly speaking, is the Divine Spirit, the shared spirit proceeding from the Father and the Son which gives expression to their unity of love. Because the opposition within the Godhead is overcome in him and (in faith) becomes visible as a presupposition of eternal love, the opposition between God and man, which is an offense to reason, can (in faith) be understood as a presupposition of the one, free, self-giving of God to his world in his Holy Spirit.[9]

Christ's work presents the opportunity for salvation to everyone, for them to join in with him in his resurrection; the Spirit provides the means by which they can make that choice. The choice is made in time but is revealed in the light of the judgment we will receive from Christ. That judgment will last, in its non-temporal experience off time, as long as necessary for someone to be transformed into the person God intends us to be. This is why, if someone goes to the judgment without any grace, they are closed in upon themselves in denial of that person God wants them to be, and they will never be transformed. For them the judgment will be never-ending. Such never-ending suffering of judgment, where time and personhood is lost, is the state of the damned, a state which God constantly strives to prevent for everyone. But will he? Balthasar did not know. He hoped that Christ accomplished his desire and all will come to the judgment with some acceptance of grace and will be saved. It might happen. This is Balthasar's hope. This is the extent of his hope. He hoped all could be saved because Christ is working with everyone, giving them all the chance for salvation, meeting them where they are at. Without seeing the outcome of the judgment, without knowing how each and every person responds to Christ, no one can know if God's work will attain his desired end, or if, through the freedom God gave us, some will turn away from God and become trapped in their rejection of God.

There is no simple universalism in Balthasar's theology. There is hope and fear; this is what is attainable on this side of the eschaton. Both need to come together. All who would declare Balthasar as a universalist ignore this paradoxical combination which Balthasar believed was all we can have, and in doing so, do his theology, his hope, a great disservice. Balthasar sought the conversion of sinners; he did not want to leave people in their sins and just assume they would be saved.

9. Balthasar, *Elucidations*, 67.

VIII

Critical Concerns Over Balthasar's Eschatology

INITIAL CONCERNS AND RESPONSES

There are many questions which can be asked concerning Balthasar's eschatology. While it is not appropriate or necessary to answer every possible question, it is important to recognize the kinds of criticism which are being given concerning his theology while offering some response to them, if feasible.[1] Even when there are legitimate concerns, it is possible to still recognize the great genius demonstrated by Balthasar's writings and to see he has offered several significant theological contributions to the Christian tradition.

In this chapter, broad questions and concerns will be brought up, and then there will be a special section to address the issues brought up by one of Balthasar's more recent critics, Ralph Martin, and what he wrote against Balthasar in his book, *Will Many Be Saved*? Martin's book has achieved some popularity and has conditioned the way many read Balthasar, which is why it is rather important to examine it and see where Martin went wrong.

Clearly, the primary question critics ask about Balthasar is whether or not he is teaching some form of *apokatastasis panton*. Many admit that

1. Only questions which are primarily eschatological in implication will be addressed.

Balthasar gave caveats to his theology, that he said he did not know whether or not all would be saved, but they think, despite words to the contrary, his theology ends up promoting universal salvation. Are they right? Sometimes, Balthasar did write in such a way that he gave strength to his critics' accusations. Yet, such texts only do so if they are read in isolation. He often will show what Christ is doing to save everyone, showing Christ will appear to everyone and meet them where they are at, but he will not describe the outcome of that meeting. Even when Christ seems to break into the wall of sin created by a sinner attached to themselves, Balthasar did not say the sinner cannot then rebuild that wall and block Christ once again from their view.[2] This is because Balthasar did not want to describe the outcome of the judgment. He believed that he was describing the theo-drama, but as the theo-drama was still at play, because it was a theo-drama he was still acting in himself, Balthasar did not know the outcome. It could be that the end of the drama will be tragic, and that some will indeed be lost.[3] In this way, the general approach many have to Balthasar, as some sort of crypto-universalist is illegitimate—only if he said the outcome was known, and that all must be saved would he be a universalist.

Nonetheless, the reason why so many will think Balthasar is a universalist is because his hope for the salvation of all permeates his work more than his discussion and fear that some might be lost. While he explained the process by which someone would be lost, it is a very generalized explanation, and he did not explain well why some, if they have already opened up to grace, would then turn against it and end up lost. Since he did not think anyone should presume they are saved, Christians who have been baptized and received grace with it could still be lost. Thus, he certainly had to think it possible that some, while initially opened up to grace can later deny it and cut themselves off from the grace they once accepted. Moreover, questions can be asked about non-Christians who have heard the Christian faith and reject it. Is it possible they accepted grace, despite such denials? Or would not their active denial of the faith assure perdition? The general structure of Balthasar's eschatology can be seen to be useful, indeed, beautiful, but its imprecision suggests that more development needs to be done so that someone can answer both of these questions before it can be accepted. This is major lacunae in his eschatology. By not wanting to determine the

2. See ET4, 456–57.

3. See TD5, 299.

outcome of the eschaton, he calls into question the significance of being a Christian.

It is not just his eschatology, but his soteriology as it relates to his eschatology, that finds criticism.[4] His discussion of Christ's descent into death contradicts the way many, if not most, Catholics understand Christ's descent into hell.[5] In his explanation, he wanted to remove any mythic understanding of that descent; that is, Balthasar did not want it to be seen as if Christ were some strongman who made a journey into the realm of the dead, risking nothing while he went, going as he did to conquer it from his own great and almighty power. Balthasar wanted to see Christ as being one of the alienated dead, indeed, as the one who experiences the greatest separation from Father as possible. This meant, to him, that Christ was like

4. Alyssa Pitstick's dissertation and book, *Light in Darkness,* is focused upon this. It is clear that her reading of Catholic tradition is narrow, possibly too narrow, and this made it difficult for her to appreciate Balthasar's thought. She makes excessive leaps in logic to find a way to criticize him. For example, she says two different creeds cannot be interpreted as being different if both are orthodox: "If the Aquileian creed is orthodox, it cannot say more than the Roman one and hence what it processes explicitly must already be implicit in the creed of Rome." Pitstick, *Light in Darkness,* 10. Of course she does not explain why a new creed cannot have something new and different from what had been said before (which is to be expected if it is produced under new circumstances). This is simply because it is not true. Creeds can reference ideas which were not thought about in other creeds, without either one being unorthodox. They can complement each other and deal with differing issues and concerns. It is this kind of logic (combined with arguments from silence) which she uses to create her own inappropriate declaration of "the catholic tradition," so that she can find a way to repudiate Balthasar. It is surprising how many have found this to be a persuasive approach. She seems incapable of appreciating the symphonic-pluralism found within Catholic theology, the kind of pluralism which allows different rites and theological traditions to find a home in the church.

5. It must be noted that theological discussions of Christ's descent into hell have always been troublesome. It is a difficult teaching to comprehend, no matter what philosophical background one holds. And yet, as Edward Oakes explained, it must be understood in relation to kenosis: "Yet given the discomfort that the doctrine of Christ's descent into hell seems to have elicited throughout the history of Christian thought, perhaps that merely indicates either an implied rejection of kenotic theology *tout court* or maybe even a rejection of *the* ultimate paradox of the Christian message: that God, the all-holy and the all-good, emptied himself not only to take on human form, but also in that human form came to know everything that rejects God, everything that is unholy, evil, and foul. Here, above all, God contradicts God." Oakes, "He Descended into Hell," 220.

Modern theology has undertaken interest in what that kenosis implies, and so is more willing to examine Christ's death in the light of kenosis; earlier descriptions of his death follow more Christ's divinity instead of his humanity, and so reflect different principles and concerns.

the rest of the dead, inactive, and indeed completely passive, awaiting the response of the Father. If this is the case, then what kind of communication does Christ really have with the dead? Steffen Lösel certainly suggested this problem when he wrote, "Curiously, Balthasar does not explain how there can be any proclamation in sheol given the fact that there is no communication among the dead."[6] The answer is that Jesus is both the one who went to the grave but also the one who rose from the grave; it is the risen Christ who meets the sinner in judgment. It is not just because he descended into death, but because he is risen, that he has become Lord of the dead.

Thus, in Balthasar's thought, the traditional way of seeing Christ amongst the dead, especially as it was often found in Christian iconography from the very beginning of church history, was recast; his descent is now seen as a continuation of and fulfillment of the kenosis begun in the incarnation. For some, this might be read as making a new myth, using a modern understanding of death as the foundation for that myth. Also, what seems like an acceptance of death and the pains associated with death might not actually be as accepting of such pains after all, because the foundation for such pain seems to be overcome in Christ.[7] For others, the notion of Christ suffering as the most "God-forsaken" of all sounds absurd because Christ is God.[8] A solution, not given by Balthasar, might be able to be had by accepting both the heroic and the suffering side of Christ are paradoxically occurring together in his descent into the dead. Humanly speaking, he is suffering as Balthasar suggests, but his divinity remains strong and engages death with the heroic victory suggested by many traditional theological

6. Lösel, "A Plain Account of Christian Salvation," 150.

7. Thus, Michele Schumacher wrote, "However, if one grants, as Balthasar insists, that God is always already reconciled—the crucifixion of Christ being proof of that (see Romans 5:6–11)—then the pain of hell that he suffers for us cannot be a revelation of our fate as sinners, or of what would have been our fate, had it not been for the salvific event. Hence, it seems arbitrary that Christ should endure hell for our salvation." Schumacher, "Representation in Balthasar," 61.

That is, if the pains of hell have been overcome, how can it be said that Christ suffered the fate of sinners when sinners do not have to suffer this fate? Of course Balthasar would say they do suffer it as long as they are under the judgment of Christ and do not cross on over to the side of Christ and into paradise. The question presumes no one suffers, but for Balthasar, all sinners suffer due to their sin. The question is not the suffering, but whether or not they will be brought out of it thanks to the accomplishment of Christ.

8. As Juan Sara explained, "The interpretation of Holy Saturday offered in tandem by Hans Urs von Balthasar and Adrienne von Speyr is often criticized for rupturing the unity of the *Logos*, with lamentable result, supposedly, of a hopeless irrationalism." Sara, "Descensus ad Inferos," 562.

models. While this might seem to divide Christ, it is not without precedent: St. Cyril of Alexandria understood that there were two different things happening to the him in his death: "He suffers in his own flesh, and not in the nature of the Godhead. The method of these things is altogether ineffable, and there is no mind that can attain to such subtle and transcendent ideas."[9]

Nonetheless, some suggest that Balthasar was borrowing too much speculation from unapproved and disputed mystical experiences, especially from Adrienne von Speyr. Indeed, for some Catholics, her views appear not to be Catholic, but Reformed, in principle, so that she was bringing, consciously or unconsciously, erroneous theological opinions which then contaminated Balthasar's theology. Nonetheless, defenders of Balthasar can point out that the so-called tradition concerning Christ's descent into the dead is not univocal, and that there are many ways notions similar to Adrienne's can be seen in historical theology. Balthasar, for example, suggested that the writings of Nicholas of Cusa and Sergius Bulgakov show he was engaging notions which were not exclusive to Protestants, even if it could be found more prevalent within some Protestant theology.[10] Likewise, Thomas White has shown that the notion that Christ suffered the pains of hell, "was taught by many Catholic thinkers in the late Middle Ages (most notably Denis the Carthusian, 1402–1471) and is present as a theme in popular preaching in Catholic Europe throughout the seventeenth, eighteenth, and nineteenth centuries (for example, in the writings of Louis Chardon, O.P., 1595–1651, and Jacques-Benigne Bossuet, 1627–1704)."[11]

Finally, Catholic thought does allow theological development which can create new paths of thinking about theological principles (as long as such development is not in contradiction to dogmatic teachings). Just because Balthasar suggested something different from others before him does not prove he is in error. Merely putting his views side by side to other such expositions proves nothing other than there are different ways which can

9. St. Cyril of Alexandria, *On the Unity of Christ,* 130.

10. Jennifer Newsome Martin's book, *Hans Urs von Balthasar and the Critical Appropriation of Russian Religious Thought,* goes at great length to show the relationship between Balthasar's thought and that coming from Russia, including notions of kenosis (see, for example, 179–85 from Martin's book). As such, Balthasar is right to say it is more than a Protestant influence, though some could suggest many of those Russian thinkers were influenced by some Protestant mystics, allowing for the chain of succession to still end with a Protestant source.

11. White, "On the Universal Possibility of Salvation," 272. In this way, while it might seem unusual, Balthasar's ideas really were not unique to him, even if what he suggested "never became the preferred theory of the church's doctrine." Ibid.

be used to discuss Christ's descent into the dead, and more needs to be done to see if any of them must be rejected.[12]

A RESPONSE TO RALPH MARTIN

One of the most recent and currently most read treatments in English on Balthasar is found in the critical work by Ralph Martin, *Will Many Be Saved.* It has received enough attention and support in some theological circles, that it is important to examine what Ralph Martin wrote, and see if a response can be given to his claims.

Martin's work properly sees evangelization is an important task of the church, but he fears that many modern eschatologies hinder such evangelization because they appear universalistic and so give little to no motivation for such evangelism. If everyone is going to be saved, why would anyone become a missionary? What would be the purpose to convert anyone to the Christian faith? Without the possibility that some, if not most, will be damned, evangelism makes little sense. There is no need for it. Salvation is already assured for all.

Martin believes that Balthasar, and Karl Rahner with him, have been misleading contemporary Christians by suggesting the possibility of universal salvation. Christians reading their works will be led to believe that there is no reason to evangelize, and so even if Balthasar and Rahner sought to glorify Christ by their work, they have inadvertently hindered Christ's work in the world.

Ralph Martin acknowledged that Balthasar did not want to be seen as a universalist. He knew Balthasar claimed all he had was the hope and not the certainly that all will be saved. For Martin, the problem is that such hope itself is too much. That hope is universalistic even if it does not intend to be. That hope will be easily misconstrued as assurance, and so once again, the purpose for evangelism will be questioned, and the missionary imperative of the church will be lost. Indeed, Balthasar and Rahner have had their writings quoted and used for the sake of such universalistic speculation:

12. This is how Edward Oakes responded to Pitstick; he pointed out that Balthasar's ideas should be seen as a possible development of Christian doctrine. He is adamant in saying they have not been rejected, and more research and exploration needs to be done before they can be accepted or rejected. Yet, Oakes did think they could help in the official Catholic exposition of doctrine in the future, believing more than likely, they are going to be seen as acceptable. See Pitstick and Oakes, "Balthasar, Hell, and Heresy," 29.

> In Catholic theology circles, as we will see, their views on the possibilities of universal salvation are cited as the basis of a prevailing consensus among Catholic theologians in favor of a strong hope that everyone may be saved and a rather skeptical attitude toward the possibility of human beings ultimately being capable of definitively saying no to the saving love of God.[13]

For Martin, the greatest problem with Balthasar is that he did not really give enough attention or seriousness to the possibility that many, if not most, will be damned. Even if Balthasar denied he was a universalist, he seemed to have hope that most will be saved. That is, Martin thought Balthasar did not take as serious as he should the thought that some could perish. Those reading Balthasar would follow through and believe there is little reason for missionary activity, for if most are going to be saved, without such evangelical efforts, it is easy to question whether or not such evangelical work will change the situation one iota.

Balthasar would not disagree with Martin's concern. If his theology was being read to suggest the likelihood that most, if not all, were going to be saved, then his theology was being misunderstood. Balthasar's hope is not on possibility or probabilities, but on the power of grace to transform people who accept it into their lives. The key is that such grace had to be accepted. For human freedom to be real, the possibility of saying no to God has to be real. While the reason why such a denial would be difficult to ascertain, that it was possible thanks to human freedom had to be acknowledged. The theo-drama had to play out, and no assumptions of the end could be made. Those who believed it was likely that all would be saved have fallen for the error of presumption. No presumption about the end, about the eschaton, which had not been revealed should be had by any Christian. The only thing which can be known is that grace can save, and those who open themselves up to God's grace will be saved. This means that the motivating factor for evangelism remains. Nonetheless, such an evangelist must keep in mind what they are doing in their work. They cannot force anyone to be saved. They cannot be assured they will convert anyone to Christ. All they can do is go out into the world and encourage others to accept Christ's offer of grace. Moreover, since everyone has a mission in the world, a calling from God, for some that calling is to be an evangelist. To deny that calling it is to deny their proper role in the world and so risk their own perdition. This is why Martin is wrong in suggesting Balthasar is

13. Martin, *Will Many Be Saved?*, 129.

disingenuous. It is fundamental to Balthasar's theology that the possibility that some will be lost be taken seriously. For Balthasar, in all actions and reactions, human freedom had to be affirmed.

It is easy to see that Ralph Martin's reading of Balthasar comes from the assumption that Balthasar is a universalist, and he reads everything Balthasar wrote in that false assumption. When he reads Balthasar, Martin ignores Balthasar's interest in human freedom, so he tries to suggest Balthasar has God overwhelm his creation, denying their freedom: "In his interpretation of Scripture and theological reasoning he is attempting to show that while we cannot deny that hell may be a *possibility*, there may indeed be no one there, so great is the power of God's love and the power of Christ's redemptive acts to overwhelm or even 'outwit' human freedom."[14]

It is true, God has the power; but for Balthasar it is not power which is the issue and which determines the outcome, but the way God opened himself to his creation with love. It is because God is love and acts with love, not self-asserting power, that God allows his creatures to determine for themselves if they will accept his love and be saved. Confusing a discussion of God's power for what God does is patently disingenuous, for if it is taken to its proper conclusion, it could be turned back on Martin and used to suggest that he denies God has the power to save everyone. Certainly, Martin would not want to say that.

Nonetheless, it is clear that Martin is trying to suggest that Balthasar's eschatology already predicts the eschaton, predicting that all or most will be saved, instead of accepting what Balthasar said which is that no one can determine the eschaton this side of the judgment. Balthasar agreed that a fatalistic form of universal salvation downplays the freedom God gave to his creation, however, he did believe God would be doing anything he could do to make a creature say yes to him. This is why Balthasar declines to say if in the end, God will lose and his hope will be unfulfilled. The refusal is not a denial that God can lose out, but a denial of the knowledge that says he necessarily will.

Because of his mistrust of Balthasar, Martin takes great effort to suggest that Balthasar's interpretation of Scripture and tradition were highly questionable, and should be rejected. For Martin, Christ's warnings of hell were not conditional, so when Balthasar suggested otherwise, Martin believes he has found one of Balthasar's biggest mistakes, and it is a mistake

14. Ibid., 136.

which he thinks tradition denies.[15] Nonetheless, by doing this, Martin is making a big mistake by trying to limit what tradition suggests to only a few examples of that tradition. He centers his understanding on what Aquinas has said. When he suggested that Aquinas provides the "permanently valid basis" for which one is to understand the riddles and paradoxes Balthasar raises, he has leveled the whole of tradition leaving only Aquinas as an authoritative source for determining theological solutions.[16] Saying this denigrates all the other theologians (and Doctors of the Church), for if they say or write or think differently than Aquinas, they are easily cast aside. It is true, someone could follow Aquinas, but it is not necessary for a theologian or believer to do so in order to be following tradition.

Likewise, Martin suggests that Balthasar was highly selective in his use of Scripture and tradition so as to stack the deck in favor of his eschatology. And yet, Martin does what he criticizes Balthasar for doing: he ends up ignoring counter-evidence in Scripture and tradition, over-simplifying such tradition to suggest to his audience that there is only one acceptable view given by tradition: his. This can be seen in the way he asks the question, "Do we know if anyone is in hell?" He thinks the answer is yes, and without much surprise, he names Judas. Balthasar, by hoping all can be saved, must suggest that Judas might not be in hell. Martin believes this response is extremely troubling and contradicts tradition.[17] After all, have not many saints and mystics suggested that Judas is in hell?[18] Nonetheless, this is not authoritative doctrine. It is not necessary to believe that Judas is in hell. Martin ignores the fact that none other than Pope John Paul II has said the church does not know the fate of Judas. In what might be a nod to Balthasar, Pope John Paul II wrote that the church must be silent on who is in hell, and that included Judas: "Even when Jesus says of Judas, the traitor, 'It would be better for that man if he had never been born' (Mt 26:24), His words do not allude for certain to eternal damnation."[19]

When pressed, Martin will admit that Balthasar might be taking up theological ideas coming from tradition. But then Martin says Balthasar at best follows a minority position in tradition, and so acts as if it is negligible.[20]

15. See Ibid., 144–45; 172–73.

16. Ibid., 173.

17. Ibid., 177.

18. Ibid.

19. Pope John Paul II, *Crossing the Threshold of Hope*, 186.

20. Martin, *Will Many Be Saved*, 139.

The proper response is not to find excuses to ignore "minority" positions in tradition, but to examine them, to delve deeper into them, to see why they even exist and what they have to offer for theological reflection today. Do they contain something which is important and yet forgotten by such neglect? Previously ignored works can be the foundation for further and deeper theological understanding. It is a kind of theological sleight of hand or circular reasoning to suggest that we follow tradition to develop our theology, but then say we choose our tradition based upon what we declare the theological tradition states *a priori* and so not allow for further development of it.

There is, in reality, a hermeneutic which Martin has taken as his own as the means by which he reads Scripture and tradition. He wants everyone else to follow him and if they do not, he criticizes them for being different. Martin has chosen particular texts as his eschatological corner-stones, and he thinks he can then demand the same for others, denying them the ability to make their choice of texts for their eschatology. Changing which texts are central to one's eschatology will create a different lens by which one reads the whole of tradition. It is a hermeneutical question, and the church does not demand one hermeneutical position for its theologians. For someone else to demand it is therefore to go beyond the expectations of the church. This, nonetheless, is what Martin does, and it for this reason, when Balthasar interprets Paul in the Book Romans in a way which Martin believes tradition rejects, he says the problem is Balthasar is not following good Scriptural hermeneutics (that is, Martin's hermeneutical key):

> Since one of the basic principles of Scriptural interpretation is that Scripture has to be interpreted in the light of Scripture it does not seem credible that this text should be understood as canceling out all the other texts of Paul and the rest of the New Testament that clearly talk about a final judgment which will result in the condemnation for whole classes of human beings. . .[21]

Nonetheless, the real problem is that Martin continuously misrepresents Balthasar, and in doing so, his criticism ends up being beside the point. Balthasar does not believe in canceling out any Scriptural texts. Interpreting them differently from Martin is not the same as cancelling them out. Indeed, Balthasar was concerned that those who deny the hope for the salvation of all are the ones neglecting Scripture, because they are trying to make Scripture present a consistent, systematic statement on the eschaton.

21. Ibid., 159.

Balthasar thought all Scriptural texts dealing with eschatology must be taken seriously, but he did this by saying they should all be seen as indicative of true possibilities, not necessities; once a particular text is turned into a necessity, other verses lose their value. Martin presumes the outcome of the eschaton, and that, Balthasar would suggest, is where Martin errs. He has turned Scripture into a fatalistic document instead of indicating the potentialities found within the eschaton.

Finally, Martin suggests that Balthasar allowed for some sort of after-death conversion, that if a sinner dies rejecting Christ, they can still be saved and repent of their sins after they have died: "Balthasar speculates that perhaps everyone will be pardoned anyway, even if they die unrepentant, or perhaps another chance will be given after death for repentance to happen, and that we should certainly hope this."[22] Yet, this is not what Balthasar proposed. While Balthasar did describe the judgment as a process of purification after death, he did not see it as some sort of after-death conversion of a sinner without any basis from their earthly life. The point for Balthasar is that what happens in the judgment of Christ follows what the person made of themselves in life. The realization of that determination is not had until the judgment, but the judgment itself is not the time for conversion. To deny this is to deny the point of purgatory, which is what Balthasar is attempting to explain with his theology of the judgment. Purgatory is not an after-death conversion, it is the purification of sins of one who has already said yes to God.

Clearly, the major concern Martin has with Balthasar's theology is that Balthasar's hope that all might be saved seems to have diminished the reasoning for missionary activity by the church.[23] Martin's commentary on Balthasar comes from his proper evangelical desires. If one believes it is likely everyone will be saved, there seems to be less motivation for evangelism, for there is little to no fear that someone would ultimately be lost. Martin believes that if the church proclaims the possibility of hell and takes it seriously, people will take the church's teaching seriously and find

22. Ibid., 180.

23. Balthasar was also concerned with evangelism, and he saw such missionary activity as a fundamental character of the church: "It [*The Razing of the Bastions*] was the realization that Jesus intended the Church to be essentially missionary in character, a community with a centrifugal movement, not a people enclosed in itself." Balthasar, *Test Everything*, 9. And, despite the features of the church, Balthasar pointed out it is one who lives a "believable imitation of Christ within the Catholic sphere" who will be successful in such activity. Ibid., 18.

a reason for conversion. Thus, fire and brimstone is a necessary part of the church's teaching if the church wants to explain why anyone should convert.[24] This is, to be sure, true—the church's teaching must include the possibility of hell, and Balthasar throughout his writings made it clear that his readers should understand this point as well. Hell must be a part of the message, despite how some might want to ignore it.[25]

The criticism Martin gave of Balthasar really is a criticism of what he believed Balthasar represented and not the actual teachings of Balthasar. Indeed, Balthasar would agree with the evangelical concerns that made Martin write as he does, but Balthasar's theology is broader in scope and is more capable of addressing evangelical concerns than Martin's simplistic approach. Balthasar did not want the Christian message to ignore the possibility of hell. Balthasar would agree with Martin that such a declaration of the faith would be dangerous. It would be a declaration of the faith which ignored the judgment and that, for Balthasar, would lead to an abolishment of the faith itself. The judgment is key. The judgment is eschatological. The judgment is to be dreaded, because perdition is possible, but the judgment is a thing of hope, because it also means sinners can be entirely freed from their sins and find salvation. Without the risk of hell, either salvation is itself lost, or human freedom is lost. For Balthasar, both had to remain. Therefore, the preaching of the faith must include the possibility of perdition, as Scripture itself warned everyone was a real, and terrible, risk. Thus, while we can have hope that all might be saved, we must not assume all will be saved. The evangelical mission remains. The possibility of hell remains. Balthasar would be among the first to say if someone rejected the possibility that some could be lost, they did not represent the Christian faith: "Thus hope for all men seems to be permitted, as long as one does not seek to anticipate the judgment of the Lord, or preach a theory of universal salvation."[26]

24. See Martin, *Will Many Be Saved?*, 131–34.

25. Balthasar understood how many in his time were questioning hell, that people were afraid to take it seriously: "Today people are afraid to use the concept of hell seriously, because it has recently been so much abused by literary people as to become quite hackneyed." Balthasar, *The God Question and Modern Man*, 119. Yet, its appearance in literature points out that hell cannot be ignored, that people intuitively know it is a real possibility to fear "We consider the fashionable interest in hell to be a symptom of a spiritual situation which cannot be overlooked, because it is so universal and constant in its expression." Ibid., 120.

26. Balthasar, *Test Everything*, 86.

While hope can be had if the judgment is not anticipated, the same is true with the possibility of hell. It remains a possibility so long as the judgment has not been made. Once it is made, it is no longer an issue of possibilities but reality. Scripture does not offer any such solution. It offers possibilities. It is for that reason that the church is right to go forth in the world, seeking to make true converts to Christ.

HOPE AND EVANGELISM

Preaching hellfire and brimstone to non-Christians, though often a popular practice of many evangelists, is not necessarily a good method for authentic missionary work. It goes too far. It will cause many to stumble when they hear such a one-sided approach to the faith. Clearly, the possibility of hell is real, and evangelism must include it. That warning does not have to be the sole focus of evangelism, nor does it have to be stated in such a way as to neglect the hope that God can find a way to bring all to salvation. For the preaching of the Gospel is more than preaching the possibility of hell, but it is also preaching the authentic Christian life, and the kind of purification all will need to go through in order to attain beatitude in Christ. It is in this respect, a preaching of hope. Without that hope, Christianity loses much of its character and risks becoming, as the then Cardinal Ratzinger stated, a "moralism" instead of the preaching the good news of Christ.[27]

Evangelism which does not allow for the hope that all might be saved ends up causing much pain and suffering to many would-be converts, because it neglects the desires of their hearts. If someone would hear it is impossible that their loved ones could be saved, they would have reason to doubt that what they are being told is good news, and so reject what they hear. They could believe God is acting underhandedly by not allowing all the chance for salvation. Evangelism is meant to meet people in all walks of life, with all kinds of hopes and dreams they might have, affirming the value of what is good, and showing how such good fits with their call to Christ. If what is good is denied, it would seem the Christian faith itself is not good. The reason why so many are attracted to the hope that all could be saved, even if they know it is unlikely, is that it presents a more attractive vision of God, for it shows God is working for everyone and not actively working for the condemnation of anyone. When such hope is entirely denied, people might lose hope for themselves and their families, leading to a loss of faith

27. Ratzinger, *Introduction to Christianity*, 250.

in God. They need the possibility that all could be saved in order to have faith in God. Without it, they could even end up believing if God exists, God is evil, and so have reason to reject God. For this reason, the argument which suggests evangelism requires the necessity that some will be lost in order to get people to convert to the faith might be true for some, but it will not be true for all, and it can provide a detriment for others who hear such a message because it will lead them to think wrongly of God. They should not be ignored just because some evangelist has an eschatological bias which others do not have.[28]

Some might end up damned. To deny this is not only to deny Scripture and tradition, but to deny human freedom. There is every possibility someone can and will continue to say no to God in perpetuity. There must be some sort of occasion where such people get what they desire, and so it must be possible some could end up damned. There is just no certainty that anyone will desire this, which is why it is impossible to know if any will be lost. This is why hope for the salvation of all is possible. It is free will that gives this hope, because it is free will which suggests there is no necessity, no determination, which has been made that determines that some will be damned. To say it is certain that some will be lost undermines human freedom. That is the problem.

Those who decry universalism usually do so because it denies free will. They say it means the outcome is already decided, and somehow or another, God will save everyone. But those who decry the hope that all might be saved are also falling for a similar determinism: they have determined

28. Balthasar noted that one of the problems of evangelization lies with the way the Gospel is preached. When it is new, or made like new, to the world, it is easier to evangelize, while it becomes increasingly difficult if people think they know the message of the Gospel and reject it. Thus, he wrote, "In the first centuries of the Christian era, the absolute newness of the message of Christ was something fascinating. In the history of the Church, this inner, essential and unsurpassable newness was experienced and lived out before the world again and again, especially by the saints. (Just think of St. Francis of Assisi) Is not the manner in which the revelation of Christ was proclaimed in modern times (on the basis of an arid Scholasticism that had become rationalistic), and perhaps the absence in many lands of great saints, a reason why this faith seems outdated?" Balthasar, *A Short Primer For Unsettled Laymen,* 16. In this way, Balthasar pointed out that evangelization is not about the mere repetition of what was said in the past. This is not a denial of the teachings of the church, but a recognition that those teachings must be kept afresh. It is only the spirit and not the mere letter of the faith which provides for true evangelization This means that evangelists can and should incorporate the hope that all might be saved in this preaching, once they found a way to incorporate it in and with the possibility that some could end up lost.

it is necessary that some will deny God. This is where Balthasar's nuance reveals its value and why he presents the best method of preaching the faith to others: his position is not universalism but hope, the hope that all will choose God. This means no one an evangelist meets will be predetermined be lost, and so there is a reason for them to evangelize everyone they should meet.

Sometimes critics of Balthasar's hope suggest the problem is that the realization of such hope is not probable. That is, they look at it as a question of probabilities and conclude the chances for such hope being fulfilled is zero. But that is not a good argument. Christians are dealing with real lives, not mere statistics. Statistics do not determine what will happen. If they did, freedom would be lost. Any talk concerning the likelihood of whether or not all will be saved is speculation and as such, is without certainty. The guesses made to establish such probabilities could be wrong. Even if and when the question is looked at as the summation of a series of probabilities, which when added together, present a possible eschatological conclusion, it is still guess work and the conclusion is most likely going to be wrong. It is fine to speculate, so long as such speculation is not taken as necessity. Some could believe that there is a great probability all will be saved, while others can consider it likely that most will be lost (as, perhaps, Augustine or those who follow him might do). Such speculation, if left as speculation, is fine, but if the probability which is made is considered a foregone conclusion, then the speculation becomes troublesome for it then reject human freedom. To speak of probabilities and turn them into necessities is look for mathematical certainties. Such certainties are never to be found when dealing with freedom. This is why the response must be agnostic. This is why it is best to hope that all might be saved and fear that some, including ourselves, might be lost.

Both the hope that all can be saved and the fear that some will be lost lies at the core of evangelism. Hope leads to evangelism because it suggests evangelism can be effective. Fear is important because it explains why evangelism is invaluable. The fear that some might reject God creates the motivation to try to reach out and make sure they do not make such a decision. Without the possibility that all might be saved or some might be damned, missionary work loses something of the Gospel. This is why Balthasar's agnostic position on the salvation of others provides the best foundation for evangelism, instead of hindering it, as some of his critics, like Ralph Martin, suggest.

IX

Concluding Remarks

HOW THIS CHAPTER WILL PROCEED

THIS CHAPTER IS DIFFERENT from the rest of the book. It is a personal reflection which engages the thought and ideas of Balthasar. In this chapter, I want to address questions which have been raised throughout the book, and address some of them based upon my own limited thoughts and intuitions. What I offer here will be brief suggestions in comparison to what has come before. They are to serve as concluding remarks which are open ended and seek to help the reader move forward and begin an engagement with Balthasar's theology on their own.

There are two aspects of Balthasar's thought I want to focus upon here.

The first of them is the role of freedom. This is as central to Balthasar's thesis as it is to those who criticize him. Both Balthasar and his critics want to address the question of freedom and both think their systematic presentations provide what is necessary for human freedom to be preserved. In this case, I believe Balthasar and his critics are both right in trying to preserve freedom but I also think Balthasar preserves the possibility of freedom in a greater sense because of his agnostic position on the eschaton. Balthasar's critics need to understand that free will and its preservation is one of the best grounds of Balthasar's hope. If someone does not agree with Balthasar's hope, it would be best for them to focus on reasons why they do so other than on the grounds of freedom.[1]

The second concern I have is that I feel his presentation on perdition is incomplete. He did a good job explaining why the possibility of perdition must be accepted, and he explored it to some degree, showing elements of the process by which someone could be damned, but the presentation is way too generalized. Balthasar left way too many lacunae for his theology to truly explain why someone would deny God and accept perdition. This is why it is easy for his critics to look at what he wrote and erroneously believe he was a universalist.

The best way to engage his theological approach to perdition is to find complementary elements from other theological sources which could be used to help explain the process of perdition. What is needed is not a rejection of what Balthasar described, but rather, the exploration and discovery of ways to add to it so that the lacunae in his theology can be filled up.

Since the purpose of this book is to explore Balthasar's theology, and not my own ideas, it is not my place to give a comprehensive complement to his theology here. Nonetheless, I feel that it would be useful to point out a way to engage his theology, suggesting how a Balthasarian based theology can develop his intuitions without neglecting his central thesis that there must be hope that all could be saved.

THE ROLE OF FREEDOM

Balthasar was no universalist. He was so concerned with the preservation of human freedom that it led him to accept that some might reject God. This was why he rejected notions of *apokatastasis*. He believed God had given everyone freedom, while universalism denied such freedom. Once God has given humanity a choice to respond to him, he would not take that choice away. He could and would do what he could to encourage people to make the right decision, but he would not make the decision for them. God did this out of love, and because of that love, he was willing to accept the decisions people made for themselves. It was a gamble that God was willing

1. For example, it is possible for some to reject the level of freedom Balthasar has given and so think, contra Balthasar, that God has a more active role in determining a person's reaction to him.

to make, because if he did not, and if he stacked the decks, his purpose for creation would have been undermined.

What exactly does free will entail? This is a philosophical question which has been asked for centuries, and will likely continue to be asked until the end of time. I have presented how Balthasar has addressed the question. Free will should not be confused with an arbitrary, indifferent freedom. Each person finds themselves put into the world with various constraints which they did not will for themselves. They did not choose where they were born. They did not choose when they were born. They did choose the casual relationships which exist in the world. While these constraints demonstrate to each person their freedom is limited, they do not undermine the reality that, after all such constraints are considered, every person still possesses a freedom of their own, a real freedom which they can use to act as they so choose. No one can act in their place. Others can try to coerce them to act in a certain way, but no one will make the choice for them, not even God.

For Balthasar, what a person wills comes with consequences. Those consequences include, but are not limited to, the transformation of the person themselves. A person's actions change them. After every act, there is a change, and after every change, they are then able to act again. This happens moment to moment, making them ever changing. In a way, they are capable to be said to be a "different person" one moment to the next. Nonetheless, no one acts as an entirely independent individual. To be in the world is to be relational. As a person acts, they either open themselves up more to others, accepting their personal nature, or they try to close themselves off, denying their personal nature, trying to become an individual apart from others.

What a person decides to do becomes a means by which they express themselves to the world. Freedom, therefore, is a gift by which someone not only decide for themselves what they will do, but it is also the gift which allows them to truly demonstrate to others, as well as to themselves, who or what they are as well as who or what they want to become, as Balthasar put so well:

> Reality gives to every entity its "to-be-what-it-is" [*in-sich-Sein*], and, in the case of a spiritual being, its "to-be-for-itself" [*für-sich-Sein*]. But at the same time it also gives every entity its "to-be-with" [*Mit-Sein*] (because every being existing in reality is real through that one reality), and in the case of a spiritual being it also gives

> it its "to-be-for-another" [*Für-ein-ander(es)-Sein*]. For that reason every being has the gift of being able to "express" itself to another, which capacity presupposes an "innerness," an ability to communicate, that is, to impart itself.[2]

While a person does not create themselves, once they have come to exist, they are free to act, to open up to God and so become co-creators with God in the establishment of their proper persona in Christ. There are conditions placed upon that activity based upon the environment they find themselves living. They cannot just wish something to happen and it happens. They have to act within the conditions which exist in the world at large. This space demonstrates to them the finitude of their existence, grounded upon the infinite freedom of God. Following Balthasar again, it can be said that all freedom, therefore, comes out of, and is related to, God's infinite freedom:

> Theologically speaking, the only thing that makes it possible to have history, in the deepest sense, within the space thus opened up is the fact that this space is an opening within the utter freedom of God (what could be more free, more completely unconditioned and grace-given, than the plan of the Incarnation and its accomplishment?); and hence that it is itself an area of freedom: freedom of God giving space and scope to the freedom of man. Within this space man is free to make history happen.[3]

However someone chooses to act, what they do can then be considered to be a positive or a negative act, that is, an act which works for or against a particular goal. For freedom to exist, this means a person must have the ability to deny what they would like to reject:

> This freedom of choice does not consist solely in preferring some elements while rejecting others, for it includes an even more remarkable element, viz., a capacity to freely ignore what cannot be worked into the edifice it constructs. The spirit can overlook completely what the senses are compelled to look at. Indeed, there is not a single apperception which does not already include such a sifting and selection. Part of the spirit's nobility is that it need not occupy itself with everything indiscriminately.[4]

2. Balthasar, *Epilogue*, 51.
3. Balthasar, *A Theology of History*, 70–71.
4. TL1, 109.

Creaturely freedom is not an absolute in itself.[5] For this reason, there is a limit to what a particular person can do; if they react negatively to the world, such negation of the world imposes limits as to what the creature can do next. Only when a person opens themselves up and allows themselves to be infused with grace can they find their freedom increasing, and with such freedom, move closer to the happiness which they naturally desire.[6] On the other hand, they can mold themselves into an objectified form, and through sin, move away from grace, and slowly start the process by which they eliminate any form of subjectivity and freedom for themselves.

In Balthasar's understanding of free will, everyone is given, as their original position on the stage of the world, a fallen mode or state of being which has left them turned away from God. They are free to continue to act in such negation of God, to continue to act turned away from God. Without God acting in their favor, without the incarnation, this turning away from God is all they would know, and so it would be all they do:

> Here we have man, both singular and plural, thrown onto the stage, endowed with freedom, condemned to freedom and given grace to exercise it, with the power of becoming what he can on the basis of his own nature and constitution and yet unable to do this outside the divine freedom but only in and with it. How sublime and yet how needy is man![7]

However, Christ has come into the world, and so he has come to meet everyone, giving everyone the chance to turn once again toward God. They are able to come face to face with God in Christ, and so to open themselves up to God in Christ, and receive the infusion of grace which will truly set them free.

In the eschatological sense, Balthasar's understanding of freedom leads us to a twofold possibility: either a person will aim to keep all they have in and of themselves, and be limited to that possession, to what they have of themselves alone, or they will deny themselves, deny their initial turning against God, and so open themselves up to God and accept his grace. That is a person will either end up with the limited potentiality they

5. See Schindler, *Hans Urs von Balthasar and The Dramatic Structure of Truth*, 198.

6. Following St. Gregory of Nyssa, Balthasar pointed out that finite freedom only finds itself fulfilled in infinite freedom, and so finite freedom seeks for and leads us to God. See TD2, 236. This is not to say it cannot get diverted: if it confuses for that end something other than God, such as the self, finite freedom can end up unfulfilled.

7. TD2, 195–96.

have in themselves for their eternity, or they will accept God beyond the self, let God in, and receive the grace they need for eternal beatitude. Hell is the end result of a will-to-the-self closed off from God. Sin is what they do to keep themselves closed off from God.

Most people, because they do not know better, embrace their initial position in the world, their initial turning away from God, as what is natural and good, and so they end up embracing that which imprisons them and makes them unhappy. Balthasar expressed how they often treat their self-made prison of sin: "This is my beloved dungeon; I yearn for no freedom! By long association I have grown fond of this prison-house of my sufferings with all of its shortcomings and all its heavy burden."[8] It is only when they realize that all they dislike is there with them in their prison is when they want to be set free from it. This is when the choice for salvation is able to be made: it is accepted when someone realizes the self-made prison they have made for themselves is what is holding them back, that so long as they maintain their false concept of who and what they are, of who and what they can become, they will never attain true glory. Only then can they accept what is necessary, the denial of that prison, the denial of that image of the self they have constructed for themselves, and turn to God.

Balthasar is clear that within the self-made prison, within a person's interior life, they are not exactly outside of God's presence. They will find God is there, encouraging them to turn to him, to give themselves over to him. This, as has been shown, is thanks to Christ's work and accomplishments in the incarnation. Now, everyone, in their very being, sees the form of Jesus coming to them, calling out to them, pleading to them, proving various ways for them to act and accept the grace which he offers them. Their calling to salvation comes not from some external evangelism, but from Jesus coming to them from within: "The form of Jesus, as form, is not attested from outside but from within."[9] God will do everything he can to show every person why they should not continue closing in on themselves, limiting themselves and going on the path toward perdition, but in the end, he still gives everyone that choice. The decision is not made by God, but by the person he is trying to entice.

Everyone is free to say no God. Despite all he does, God will not force a yes from his creature, he will not force someone to deny themselves and accept his saving grace. Each denial of God and the good he offers to the

8. HW, 141.

9. GL1, 605.

person closes off that good; it is lost forever. It will not be offered again, for it is lost with the passing of time. If a person accepts some good, some grace, it gives God the chance to offer new, similar goods, new means to open the person up. They can still deny God again, and destroy the good within, so that the mere acceptance of some good at one point is not enough to save them. It is only when they have entirely opened up to God will they be saved. On the other hand, if someone closes off every avenue God uses to try to entice them to say yes, if every time God tries to use some good in the world as a means of enticing a person to say yes to him, in the end, there will be nothing left for him to lead the person to him, and so that person will be lost.

Freedom can therefore be used, paradoxically, to destroy itself; the more a person freely denies the good outside of themselves, the less free they become. Finally, the freedom to say yes to God can be eliminated. When this happens, there is nothing left but a continuous no to God. They become purely objectified images of denial, with their subjective freedom entirely lost, and so all others see them in and through that no, in and through that denial of God. Their image is the image of an immobile negation to God. It is stuck in a cycle self-attachment, with the creation and identification of the self produced by their actions as being all they shall ever want to will for and attain.

Freedom, therefore, has the seed of its own destruction within it. This is why freedom, while good, can still lead someone away from the good and to sin. Freedom ultimately is the determination to either open up in love, to be a free persona interacting with all, allowing oneself to be constantly changing for the better (*theosis*), or the rejection of all such grace and improvement through the denial of all such love and therefore making for oneself the hateful attachment to that self as all one does forever. Freedom can account for sin, for it is only in the free will that sin can be chosen.

HABITS

To be saved, everyone must open themselves up to God, making room for him and his grace into their very person. While this aspect of his theology makes a lot of sense, I fear that Balthasar does not do a good job explaining why someone would not do so. It is easy to understand why, initially, some might deny God, but why, if he is continuously there working to save someone, will someone deny him once they have seen the mess they have made for themselves and their limited freedom?

Balthasar was right to suggest that God is doing everything he can do to get everyone to say yes to him, using everything at his disposal for the sake of eliciting that yes. There is nothing wrong with the suggestion that God might even use our bondage to sin in a way to show us his glory and elicit a yes from him, so long as it is understood God is not accepting sin and calling sin good, but that he is using the condition established by sin to suggest to the sinner something better could be theirs if they but say yes to him.[10]

Whatever decision someone makes for or against God, it will come from the whole of their experience and so the whole of their existence. Their reaction to Christ in his judgment of them and their sin will be based upon what they did in their lives, what decisions they made for or against God during their lives. It is important to emphasize that the judgment reveals the character of a person, and what they have made of themselves in their lives, and is not a time or place for conversion. It is not a second chance to say yes to God, but the time in which everyone is shown whether or not we have made that yes, and if they have done so, it is the time in which God draws it out from all the negativity and sin which might otherwise hide it from the person being judged.[11]

Thus, while Balthasar believed it possible that some could be eternally lost, and it will be revealed at the judgment if they are, there remains the question as to who this person would be, and why they would deny God. Every time Balthasar provides a description of what could lead someone to perdition, it always seems as if he has a way out, a loophole which leaves it open that the one who would otherwise be lost, will still be saved. This is not because Balthasar wanted to establish a universalistic eschatology, but rather, because he wanted to leave the possibility open that anyone who is among the living is not yet judged and condemned. He wanted to present how someone could be lost, but because he did not know if anyone would be lost, he did not entirely know or understand the subjectivity which would lead someone to deny God.

Hell is the objectification of a subject, rendering them no longer a subject, and so, no longer free. Condemnation is the judgment which is

10. See Balthasar, *Does Jesus Know Us*, 30.

11. Balthasar expressed this point will be writing, "In eternity you will live as that which you have been." HW, 30.

rendered upon us as objects. Until that judgment, God is constantly at work, trying to stop the sinner from becoming purely objective (explaining the "ways out of perdition" constantly seen in Balthasar's work). The lost sinner is the one who is completely objectified and stuck in the objectivity of sin. How exactly did they get there? What could have been said or done to prevent such full objectivity?

The subjective dimension of perdition, though touched upon in Balthasar's works, remains the best place for further theological exploration. There is room to develop Balthasar's intuitions with examinations on the kinds of psychological and spiritual conditionings which might lead someone to reject God, indeed, to see how and why someone willingly loses their own freedom. That is, a proper psychological analysis can offer a complementary analysis, giving possible answers to questions Balthasar did not dare ask or answer. Through psychology it is possible to see how and why people become addicted to harmful things like drugs which they know will harm them and yet they do so nonetheless. Psychology can explain why people would act in the world in a way which leads them away from the happiness and joy they desire out of life. That is, psychology can show, in and through real subjects, what makes people act contrary to their own best interests, destroying themselves in the process. Once this is understood, it would be possible to see then if this has some similarity to why some could deny God and so willingly accept perdition.

This is not to suggest Balthasar has completely ignored the psychological side of sin. He did explore it in part, but when he did so, it was merely a small portion of the psyche which he exposed, not the whole of it. Perhaps the best examination Balthasar wrote on the "psychology" of sin is found in the small book, *The Christian and Anxiety*, and even then, it hints at a lot, but does not give us enough to explain why a sinner would truly keep to their own sin and deny God. Within it, the best description he provides of his analysis, simplifying it in one sentence, is to say, "The sinner wants to stand on his own, not on God."[12]

Sinners, standing alone against God, will find themselves stumbling around in the world. When they fall, when they reach to the depth of the despair due to their own inability to be all they want to be by themselves, will they remain to themselves or will they let God in and save them? The answer is not known, but what is interesting is that Balthasar pointed out that such anxiety and fear, such dread that the sinners feel, can be the

12. Balthasar, *Christian and Anxiety*, 100.

condition either for the sinner's repentance or for them to continue further in their denial of God, creating, as it were, a closed loop of sin, where one sin becomes the precondition for the next, and the next, without end if the sinner uses it to continuously deny God:

> The anxiety of the wicked is an anticipation of the darkness of Hades, and the light within it is deceptive, for the anxiety is a lasting condition, while the anxiety of good men is a process, a passage, an episode between light and light. The anxiety of the wicked is both effect and cause of their turning away from God; it encloses and incarcerates; it is the sign of God's wrath set up over them—whereas the anxiety of the good has as its meaning and purpose to open them up to God in their cry for mercy; it is the banner of God's grace unfurled over them.[13]

Here, once again, Balthasar at once becomes suggestive, giving as close an examination as he can of what will lead a sinner to perpetually deny God, but then he does not find it possible to leave it at that. He sees the same condition which allows the sinner to deny God becomes the means by which they can also affirm him. Anxiety for Balthasar has two modalities: that of the wicked and that of the good. Nonetheless, he suggests something quite important: sin can become a self-made cycle which entraps the sinner and keeps them turned away from God.

Similarly, in his *Theo-logic,* he considered the notion of that we all have an "evil instinct."[14] It is something within us which encourages us to sin. What Balthasar has in mind here is the concept of concupiscence. The flesh, with its impulses and desires, can encourage a person to give in those impulses at the wrong times; there is, in theory, no limit to what the flesh can desire, and so the instinct which it can provide to the person acting in the world. The key is for a person to control those instincts, to find the proper balance for their use, so that they are not to be seen as evil, but needing proper guidance. If a person is too attached to their flesh, to their bodies, and what they offer, it is possible for them to use it to turn away from God and to become attached to themselves; this is why it can be seen as a major source for sin, while it is not itself evil.[15] For example, gluttons

13. Ibid., 67.

14. TL2, 320.

15. See TL2, 323. Balthasar pointed out that the law was meant to put the desires of the flesh in check, but was incapable of doing so. Only by the incarnation, by the Son taking on the flesh and letting the flesh come to its proper end in the death of Christ, can the flesh and its instincts come to an end, so that now, after the cross, we can "crucify the flesh" and overcome its dictates. TL2, 324.

begin by eating normally, but get enticed by food and the pleasures they receive by eating; they slowly become consumed by their own pleasures, and end up trapped in a cycle of perpetual hunger, finding no final satisfaction when they gorge themselves with food. The instinct to eat is good, and a necessary part of life, but when it becomes not just a tool for existence but the end all for a person's being, then such attachment turns into a sin which keeps someone turned away from God and turned within themselves. The same can be said of other instincts, other natural desires; when a person turns the practice of such instincts into goals, they become the slaves of their instincts, losing elements of their personal freedom as result.

While Balthasar addressed the anxiety of the wicked, and the instinct we have within which can turn us away from God and sin, he did not address either of them in depth. He saw how they could connect to perdition, but he was more concerned to see how God can work beyond these problems and find a way to save sinners. As such, while giving a nod to these issues, Balthasar left them only at their initial forms of investigation. He has left room for others to explore them further, and from such a means, possibly understand better why someone would remain attached to sin and so deny grace forever for themselves.

What I would suggest could be done is that we take to what Balthasar has discussed on the notion of anxiety and instincts, and look at them with under the lens of the category of habits. Taking texts, such as St. Thomas Aquinas' *Summa Theologica*,[16] it is possible to discuss how habits of the will are formed. Then we can appropriate this wisdom to Balthasar's theology and end up suggesting that the will to deny God is itself a habit which a sinner creates for themselves. If the habit is not overturned in life, then it follows a person in their death to the judgment seat of Christ, and forms the basis of the sinner's no to God in their judgment.

A useful definition for what is meant by a habit is found in John Elmendorf's *Elements of Moral Theology*:

> What is a habit? A representative text on the topic defines it simply as: A habit is a (fixed) quality or disposition of our soul, whereby we are well or ill regulated, either in ourself or relatively to something else. (Arist. Met. v. 25.) Habits stand between our active powers and their operations. For, by their definition, they have a two-fold relation: on one side to the subject of them; on the other

16. Aquinas, *Summa Theologica*, I-II Q.49–54.

> side, to the end of that subject, which is its activity, its operation, as either the end, or leading to the end.[17]

A habit, therefore, points to a disposal of the will by a person, a disposal which makes them normally act in accord with it as their particular end. This disposition can become fixed, it can be given by God through grace, or it can be established as the end product of other willful activities. A person can create dispositions, habits, by their actions, and this is central to the engagement of the concept of the habit with Balthasar's theology. The point is that a person creates, through their actions, who they think themselves to be, a concept of the self, which then directs and guides them in future actions; when it becomes reified, it becomes a habit, and when the habit itself becomes all-consuming, it then destroys the person and closes them off from the grace of God.

If we know how we create habits, we can find a way to overcome them. Perdition can be said to be the end result of a habitual rejection of God. What would lead a person to reject God habitually? They create and hold on to a false concept of the self over and above God's mission for themselves. This false self is allowed to rule and guide them in their actions. When they ignore God and focus only on this self, this false representation of themselves, this is how and why they can create a habit which conditions their own damnation. By understanding this promotion of the self as a kind of habit, we have a new way to address sinners and their rejection of God. To be sure, to explore this matter properly, a new study would have to be done, taking on the theology of habits from a wide range of spiritual sources. What I am interested in here is positing a way to engage Balthasar which will allow for a better understanding of perdition; whether such an endeavor will end up with a better result than by talking about Balthasar alone is not known, but it seems likely to me.

Looking at sin as a habit instead of an instinct will prevent any assumption that instincts in us are evil, and it will also suggest that sin is capable of being overcome because it is a habit and not an instinct. Nonetheless, in a general sense, when a person has become accustomed to their habits, they might have a difficult time distinguishing their habits from their instincts, and will think their habit is also an instinct which is a part of them. This is why so many can confuse a habit for nature, for they confuse the habit they have developed for a natural instinct which must therefore be good. Sin must never be seen as something natural or good. Sin can never be a part

17. Elmendorf, *Elements of Moral Theology*, 58.

of human nature; it serves to corrupt it, and in and through the creation of habits, the false sense of self demonstrates the overlay sin creates and why it looks like it is natural but it is not.

While there are many bad habits which someone can possess (or be possessed by), it is important to point out, we can consider the existence of an over-arching habit which moves a person to establish a vision of the self and their understanding of themselves. We can call this the root habit of sin, which emerges from original sin and yet is different from it (since original sin can be cleansed from a person while this habit remains). Habits are a basis by which the constructed, false-image of the self is produced, for they merge together with this root habit, to be the foundation for the sense of self which the habit then tries to hold to and defend against all which would eliminate it. This root habit would be the means by which the false-self is constructed, the false-self which must be rejected and denied if someone is to say yes to God. Yet, since the self is changing, the habit itself can be said to be changing, so that the new image of the self after an act will create a new form of attachment promoted by the root habit. The two go together, and form a cycle in which the false self can then encourage the formation of new habits when then further suggests new notions of the self. So long as the habit is left unopposed, this can create a perpetual loop, the kind which is necessary for perdition because perdition itself is the continuous denial of God for the affirmation of the constructed image of the self. This root habit, so long as we live, is in flux; elements can be added to it, and elements removed from it; as someone tries to open up to God, God's grace can come in and help them overturn bad habits, freeing themselves from the falsely constructed image of the self, and so slowly eliminate the root habit which merges from them; but if they have deny grace, and affirm the self apart from God, then the habit will be reinforced, until at last, it could become perpetual and a person truly has become objectified in their existence by their own force of habit.

It is possible for someone to fight against a reification of a false sense of self where they seek the transcendent good while failing to overcome any so-called minor habits of sin. They are turning to God, saying yes to God, and receiving grace from God. Often the effects of that grace will appear to be slowly working in them, slowly working for their sanctification. Its presence will be manifested, but only properly and completely employed in death, in the judgment, where their bad habits will finally be able to be cast off on Christ and they will be able to become the person God intended them to be and they will be saved. On the other hand, those who come to the judgment with no grace, those who have not denied themselves and their habits but have always sought to affirm them over God, will have nothing within to save them and so they will be those who suffer perdition.

The bad habit which binds a sinner in to their false sense of the self is seeded and strengthened by all sin. It can even be seeded by apparent virtues, if someone were try to embrace them and use them to identify themselves as being good by them while staying distant from and denying the grace of God. As long as someone holds on to themselves and denies the grace of God to help them let go of their false image of themselves, that false self will be strengthened and solidified by their continual hold on themselves; their own grip upon themselves is their own imprisonment. On the other hand, even the littlest opening to God, even the most minor of yeses to him, can create cracks in the foundation of the false-self, and be used to bring a person to salvation.

The key, then, is to see the spiritual battle going on in each and every person. It is manifested in their habits, but because the internal disposition to them is not known, whether or not the bad habits are going to lead to perdition or not is not known. What is known is that they can be used to reinforce the general root habit which seeks to have a person remain totally self-enclosed by their own attachment to themselves.

A theology of habits which sees that there is a foundational habit for sin, a habit which motivates someone to turn toward a false sense of self apart from God, can accept Balthasar's understanding of the problem of grasping for the self apart from God, but it will do so with the recognition that this grasping is a process in continual flux and capable of being modified unless it is solidified in eternity. It can see that there is an overarching habit to self-attachment which must be overcome, but it does so warning that the way to do so is not through the creation of another, similar habit, but by overturning the habit itself and opening up to God apart from the self. If a person lets God direct them to their proper end, instead of struggling to create and identify it for themselves, God can then lead the person to beatitude.

Understanding this, then, can suggest new ways of evangelism. Evangelism should be based upon bringing a person to Christ, so that they open themselves to Christ and let his grace purify them and make them to be the person God wants out of them. Evangelists can also consider how they can help make this possible by looking at the habits each particular person has developed, and see if there is a need for them to be overturned. If there is, then they can help such a person do so—always reminding them that as they do so, they are to do so with grace, in cooperation with God, and not a part from it.

In this fashion, a theology of habits can take Balthasar at his word, and take his theology of perdition seriously, but also consider the implications of that theology in relation to real people who could truly decide for themselves to deny God forever. It suggests why they could do so, even if and when God offers them the opportunity for salvation. They have reified their no to God by turning it into a habit.

Balthasar did not want to go into depth with the psychology of sin. Balthasar had a good reason for this. He was concerned that such talk could undermine any turn toward grace. Why? Because psychology, and many forms of spirituality, all aim for "technique" to help people get better, but such technique ends up being self-reifying, as forming ways to ratify a higher form of self apart from God. Technique alone is not good enough. "What is essential, however, is not a confidently mastered technique but surrender of the self to that which God in his love bestows on those who firmly believe in him."[18] Without God, such techniques would end up leading to temporary peace, distracting a person from their true spiritual problems as they reify a new form of the self which would lead them slowly to hell. Such techniques, by themselves, do not address the true need, the need to embrace Christ and suffering in Christ which leads to our purification; this is what Balthasar believed was the problem with Asian spirituality: "Asia attempts to overcome the oppositions of matter through a technique of the spirit, but it must be said in Christian terms that the path to the birth of the 'new person in accordance with God' was not a state free of all suffering, *apatheia*, but Christ's suffering to the full all guilt unto death."[19] In this manner, would not what I suggest about habits counter what Balthasar explained?

To respond to this, it is important to remember, Balthasar did not have a problem with spiritual practices and meditation. What he feared was the embrace of such techniques which led a person to think their salvation came from within and what they did for themselves. They should be used in

18. Balthasar, *Test Everything*, 28.

19. ET3, 497.

relation to grace, not a part from it, to open up a person to God, not to find their solution to their problems within. He saw how many could and did use spiritual practices as promoting a fantasy of self-made goodness, following the errors of Pelagius. This is why the elimination of particular bad habits is not necessarily indicative of grace, if the habit of self-attachment which closes oneself off from God remains. Techniques can eliminate bad habits, but only the detachment of the person from their false concept of the self and the opening of themselves up to God is what will bring them salvation. Balthasar is concerned with those who confuse the spiritual techniques as if the techniques themselves necessarily established grace; but when used properly, they can open up a person and make them ready for such grace.

Balthasar, despite his fears that such techniques can lead someone astray, still preserved with that criticism the hope that all could be saved. His criticism concerning spiritual or psychological techniques must not be seen outside of that hope. All that is good with their practice will notbe rejected by God, and such techniques can help people start on the path toward God. Such techniques, when applied prudentially, can help people trapped in particular vices get out of them, and slowly weaken the habit which turns them in upon themselves and away from God.

WHERE WE CAN GO FROM HERE

I believe the best thing Balthasar provided to the Christian faith is his hope. He hoped all can be saved. No one, while they are still living, has been lost to God. This is a necessary foundation for any legitimate missionary activity. It means that there is always a chance for success. Balthasar reminds us that everyone we meet has a potential for being saved. Even those who appear to be the worst of sinners can still be saved; it just takes the person to open themselves up to God and to allow God to do the rest. Even the smallest opening to God is enough for God to work with the person and transform them into the person he wants them to be. Balthasar's hope is the hope that even apparent failure can turn into victory for God.

Having, therefore, presented my vision of how Balthaasar's theology can be adapted, it now can be asked, where do we go from here? We follow Balthasar's general intuitions, even if we adapt them to make sure they can better appreciate why someone could choose against God. We go with that hope. We hope that everyone we encounter can be saved. We hope we can help everyone we meet, and show to them by our lives the true value of a

Christian life so that they can be motivated by it and slowly be transformed by Christ themselves. The Christian witness is the witness of Christ in our lives, and how he has helped us become something more than we were without him. We know God can help others because he has helped us in ourselves. The more we let Christ transform us, the more we are able to provide that hope to others, and the greater the chance we might be successful in encouraging others to follow after Christ as well.

We must witness to others the work of Christ in our lives. We must find a way to embrace hope and not despair, but we must also understand the path which leads to hell, the kinds of actions people can take while on it, so as to warn them of their possible end. That is why we must seek to understand perdition even if we remain in hope. We must understand the potential for damnation, and what would lead someone to reject Christ, if we want to suggest a way around such perdition.

We can therefore follow Balthasar and turn ourselves completely over to Christ. We must live with Christ. We should follow him where he would lead us. We follow him in love, and with such love, love all those we encounter in the world. For it is in such love the light grace is able to shine in the world, the light which has the power to save all if everyone agrees to its direction. Balthasar's significance is that he reminds us of this hope. Having embraced it, we can move beyond theory and follow Jesus wherever he would have us go, hoping that we will be open to follow him even to hell and back, if that is what is necessary for us to be saved.

Bibliography

Ackerman, Stephan. "The Church as Person in the Theology of Hans Urs von Balthasar." *Communio* 29 (2002) 238–49.

Aquinas, St. Thomas. *Summa Theologica*. Translated by Fathers of the English Dominican Province. New York: Benzinger Brothers, 1947.

Babini, Ellero. "Jesus Christ, Form and Norm of Man According to Hans Urs von Balthasar." *Communio* 16 (1989) 446–57.

von Balthasar, Hans Urs. *Apokalypse der deutschen Seele: Studien zu einer Lehre von letzen Haltunger*. Einsiedel: Johannes Verlag, 1998.

———. *A Theology of History*. San Francisco: Ignatius, 1994.

———. *The Christian and Anxiety*. Translated by Dennis D. Martin and Michael J. Miller. San Francisco: Ignatius, 2000.

———. *The Christian State of Life*. Translated by Sister Mary Frances McCarthy. San Francisco: Ignatius, 1983.

———. *Cosmic Liturgy: The Universe According to Maximus the Confessor*. Translated by Brian E. Daley, SJ. San Francisco: Ignatius, 2003.

———. *Dare We Hope "That All Men Be Saved?" With A Short Discourse on Hell*. Translated by Dr. David Kipp and Rev. Lothar Krauth. San Francisco: Ignatius, 1988.

———. *Does Jesus Know Us? Do We Know Him?* Translated by Graham Harrison. San Francisco: Ignatius, 1983.

———. *Elucidations*. Translated by John Riches. San Francisco: Ignatius, 1998.

———. *Engagement with God*. Translated by R. John Halliburton. San Francisco: Ignatius, 1986.

———. *Epilogue*. Translated by Edward J. Oakes, SJ. San Francisco: Ignatius, 2004.

———. *Explorations in Theology I: The Word Made Flesh*. Translated by A.V. Littledale and Alexander Dru. San Francisco: Ignatius, 1989.

———. *Explorations in Theology IV: Spirit and Institution*. Translated by Edward J. Oakes, SJ. San Francisco: Ignatius, 1995.

———. "The Fathers, the Scholastics, and Ourselves." *Communio* 24 (1997) 347–96.

———. *First Glance at Adrienne von Sepyr*. Translated by Antje Lawry and Sr. Sergia Englund, O.C.D. San Francisco: Ignatius, 1981.

———. *The Glory of the Lord: A Theological Aesthetics*. 7 vols. Translated by Eramso Leiva-Merikakis, et al. San Francisco: Ignatius, 1982.

———. *The God Question and Modern Man*. Translated by Hilda Graef. Eugene, OR: Wipf and Stock, 2000.

———. *Heart of the World*. Translated by Erasmo S. Leiva. San Francisco: Ignatius, 1979.

———. *In the Fullness of Faith: On the Centrality of the Distinctively Catholic.* Translated by Graham Harrison. San Francisco: Ignatius, 1988.

———. *The Laity and the Life of the Counsels: The Church's Mission in the World.* Translated by Brian McNeil, C.R.V, and D.C. Schindler. San Francisco: Ignatius, 2003.

———. *Love Alone is Credible.* Translated by D.C. Schindler. San Francisco: Ignatius, 2004.

———. *Man in History: A Theological Study.* Translated by William Glen-Doepell. London: Sheed and Ward, 1982.

———. *The Moment of Christian Witness.* Translated by Richard Beckley. San Francisco: Ignatius, 1994.

———. *Mysterium Paschale.* Translated by Aidan Nichols. Grand Rapids, MI: Eerdmans, 1993.

———. *My Work in Retrospect.* Translated by Brian McNeil C.R.V. San Francisco: Ignatius, 1993.

———. *New Elucidations.* Translated by Sister Mary Theresilde Skerry. Ignatius: San Francisco, 1986.

———. *Our Task.* Translated by Dr. John Saward. San Francisco: Ignatius, 1994.

———. *A Short Primer For Unsettled Laymen.* Translated by Michael Waldstein. San Francisco: Ignatius, 1985.

———. *Test Everything: Hold Fast To What Is Good.* Translated by Maria Shrady. San Francisco: Ignatius, 1989.

———. *Theo-Drama: Theological Dramatic Theory.* 5 vols. Translated by Graham Harrison. San Francisco: Ignatius, 1988–1998.

———. *Theo-Logic.* 3 vols. Translated by Adrian J. Walker and Graham Harrison. San Francisco: Ignatius, 2000–2005.

———. *The Theology of Karl Barth.* Translated by Edward T. Oakes, SJ. San Francisco: Ignatius, 1992.

———. *Truth is Symphonic: Aspects of Christian Pluralism.* Translated by Graham Harrison. San Francisco: Ignatius, 1987.

———. *You Crown the Year With Your Goodness.* Translated by Graham Harrison. San Francisco: Ignatius, 1989.

———. *You Have Words of Eternal Life.* Translated by Dennis Martin. San Francisco: Ignatius, 1991.

von Balthasar, Hans Urs and Adrienne von Speyr. *To The Heart of the Mystery of Redemption.* Translated by Anne Englund Nash. San Francisco: Ignatius, 2010.

Barbarin, Msgr. Philippe. *Théologie et Sainteté.* Paris: CERP, 1999.

Barron, Robert. "A Reflection on Christ, Theological Mood, and Freedom." In *How Balthasar Changed My Mind,* edited by Rodney A. Howsare and Larry S. Chapp, 9–25. New York: Herder & Herder, 2008.

Baumer, Iso. "Die Relevanz der orthodoxen Theologie für die Theologie von Hans Urs von Balthasar." In *Logik der Liebe und Herrlichkeit Gottes: Hans Urs von Balthasar im Gespräch (FS für K. Lehmann),* edited byWalter Kasper, 229–56. Ostfildern: Mathias Grünewald Verlag, 2006.

Birot, Antoine. "'God in Christ, Reconciled the World to Himself': Redemption in Balthasar." In *Communio* 24 (1997) 259–85.

Blankenhorn, Bernhard OP. "Balthasar's Method of Divine Naming." In *Nova et Verera* 1 (2003) 245–68.

Block, Ed Jr. "Introduction." In *Glory, Grace and Culture: The Work of Hans Urs von Balthasar,* edited by Ed Block Jr., 1–15. New York: Paulist, 2005.

St. Bonaventure. *Breviloquium.* Translated by Erwin Esser Nemmers. St. Louis, MO: B. Herder Book Company, 1946.

Bonnici, John S. *Person to Person: Friendship and Love in the Life and Theology of Hans Urs von Balthasar.* New York: Alba House, 1999.

Carpenter, Anne. "Theo-Poetics: Figure and Metaphysics in the Thought of Hans Urs von Balthasar." PhD. diss., Marquette University, 2012.

Cavanaugh, William T. "Balthasar, Globalization, and the Problem of the One and the Many." In *Communio* 28 (2001) 324–47.

Cihak, John. *Balthasar and Anxiety.* London: T&T Clark, 2009.

Cirelli, Anthony Tyrus Gaines. "Form and Freedom: Patristic Revival and the Liberating Encounter between God and Man in the thought of Hans Urs von Balthasar." PhD. dissertation, The Catholic University of America, 2007.

Sacred Congregation for the Doctrine of Faith. *Epistola de quibusdam quaestionibus ad Eschatologiam spectantibus.* http://www.vatican.va/roman_curia/congregations/cfaith/documents/rc_con_cfaith_doc_19790517_escatologia_en.html.

Crawford, David S. "Love, Action, and Vows as 'Inner Form' of the Moral Life." In *Communio* 32 (2005) 295–312.

St. Cyril of Alexandria. *On the Unity of Christ.* Translated by John Anthony McGuckin. Crestwood, NY: St Vladimir's Seminary, 1995.

Daley, Brian E. "Balthasar's Reading of the Church Fathers." In *The Cambridge Companion to Hans Urs von Balthasar,* edited by Edward T. Oakes, SJ, and David Moss, 187–206. Cambridge: Cambridge University Press, 2004.

Dalzell, Thomas G. *The Dramatic Encounter of Divine and Human Freedom in the Theology of Hans Urs von Balthasar.* New York: Peter Lang, 2000.

Denzinger, Heinrich. *The Sources of Catholic Dogma.* Translated by Roy J. Deferrari. St. Louis, MO: B. Herder Book Company, 1957.

Dickens, W. T. "Balthasar's Biblical Hermeneutics." In *The Cambridge Companion to Hans Urs von Balthasar,* edited by Edward T. Oakes, SJ, and David Moss, 175–86. Cambridge: Cambridge University Press, 2004.

Donnelly, Veronica. *Saving Beauty: Form As the Key to Balthasar's Christology.* Bern: Peter Lang, 2007.

Dupré, Louis. "The Glory of the Lord: Hans Urs von Balthasar's Theological Aesthetic." In *ans Urs von Balthasar: His Life and Work,* edited by David L. Schindler, 183–206. San Francisco: Ignatius, 1991.

———. "Hans Urs von Balthasar's Theology of Aesthetic Form." In *Theological Studies* 48 (1988) 299–318.

Elmendorf, John J. *Elements of Moral Theology.* New York: James Pott & Company, 1892.

Enders, Markus. "'Alle weltliche Schönheit is fur den antiken Menschen die Epiphanie göttlicher Herrlichkeit.' Zur vorchristlichen Wahrnehmung des Schönen in der heidnischen Antike nach Hans Urs von Balthasar." In *Logik der Liebe und Herrlichkeit Gottes. Hans Urs von Balthasar im Gespräch (FS für K. Lehmann),* edited by Walter Kasper, 26–44. Ostfildern: Mathias Grünewald Verlag 2006.

Fields, Stephen, SJ. "Balthasar and Rahner on the Spiritual Senses." In *Theological Studies* 57 (1996) 224–41.

Franks, Angela Franz. "Trinitarian *Analogia Entis* in Hans Urs von Balthasar." In *The Thomist* 62 (1998) 533–59.

Gardiner, Anne Barbeau and Jacques Servais. "Correcting the Deposit of Faith? The Dubious Adrienne von Speyr." In *New Oxford Review* 69 (2002) 31–45.

Gawronski, Raymond, SJ. *Word and Silence: Hans Urs von Balthasar and the Spiritual Encounter between East and West.* Edinburgh: T&T Clark, 1995.

Gonzalez, Michelle A. "Hans Urs von Balthasar and Contemporary Feminist Theology." In *Theological Studies* 65 (2004) 566–95.

Hadley, Christopher, SJ. "The All-Embracing Frame: Distance in the Trinitarian Theology of Hans Urs von Balthasar." PhD. diss., Marquette University, 2015.

Harrison, Victoria S. "Putman's Realism and von Balthasar's Religious Epistemology." In *International Journal for Philosophy of* Religion 44 (1998) 67–92.

Healy, Nicholas J. *The Eschatology of Hans Urs von Balthasar: Being as Communion.* Oxford: Oxford University Press, 2005.

Henrici, Peter, SJ. "Hans Urs von Balthasar: A Sketch of His Life." In *Hans Urs von Balthasar: His Life and Work,* edited by David L. Schindler, 7–44. San Francisco: Ignatius, 1991.

Hofer, Andrew, OP. "Balthasar's Eschatology on the Intermediate State." In *Logos* 12 (2009)148–72.

The Holy Bible. Revised Standard Version. Philadelphia: Westminster, 1952.

Holzer, Vincent. "Figure et Kénose chez Balthasar." In *Revue des Sciences Religieuses* 79 (2005) 249–78.

Howsare, Rodney. *Balthasar: A Guide For the Perplexed.* London: T&T Clark, 2009.

———. *Balthasar and Protestantism.* London: T&T Clark, 2005.

Hunt, Anne. *The Trinity and the Paschal Mystery: A Development in Recent Catholic Theology.* Collegeville, MN: Liturgical, 1997.

Saint Ignatius of Loyola. "The Spiritual Exercises." In *Saint Ignatius of Loyola: Personal Writings.* Translated by Joseph A. Munitiz and Philip Endean. New York: Penguin, 1996.

International Theological Commission. *Some Current Questions In Eschatology (1992). http://www.vatican.va/roman_curia/congregations/cfaith/cti_documents/rc_cti_1990_problemi-attuali-escatologia_en.html.*

Pope John Paul II. *Crossing the Threshold of Hope.* Translated by Jenny McPhee and Martha McPhee. New York: Alfred A. Knopf, 1994.

———. *Fides et Ratio.* Vatican Translation. Boston: Pauline Books & Media, 1998.

———. *Veritatis Splendor.* http://www.vatican.va/holy_father/john_paul_ii/encyclicals/documents/hf_jp-ii_enc_06081993_veritatis-splendor_en.html .

Johnson, Kenneth K. "*Analogia Entis*: A Reconsideration of the Debate Between Karl Barth and Roman Catholicism, 1914–1968." PhD. diss., Princeton Theological Seminary, 2008.

Johnson, Keith L. "Erich Przywara's Early Version of the Analogy of Being." In *Princeton Theological Review* 40 (2009) 9–22.

———. *Karl Barth and the Analogia Entis.* London: T&T Clark, 2010.

Kuzma, Andrew John. "Theo-Dramatic Ethics: A Balthasarian Approach to Moral Formation." PhD. diss., Marquette University, 2016.

Levering, Matthew. "Balthasar on Christ's Consciousness on the Cross." In *The Thomist* 65 (2001) 567–81.

Lococo, Donald J. "Freedom and Intimacy in von Balthasar's Theo-logic 1." In *Analecta Hermeneutica* 1 (2009) 114–35.

Long, D. Stephen. *Saving Karl Barth: Hans Urs von Balthasar's Preoccupations*. Minneapolis, MN: Fortress, 2014.

López, Antonio. "Eternal Happening: God as an Event of Love." In *Love Alone is Credible: Hans Urs von Balthasar as Interpreter of the Catholic Tradition,* edited by David L. Schindler, 75–104. Grand Rapids, MI: Eerdmans, 2008.

Lösel, Steffen. "A Plain Account of Christian Salvation? Balthasar on Sacrifice, Solidarity and Substitution." *Pro Ecclesia* 13 (2004) 141 -171.

———. "Conciliar, not Conciliatory: Hans Urs von Balthasar's Ecclesiological Synthesis of Vatican II." In *Modern Theology* 24 (2008) 23–49.

———. "Love Divine, All Love Excelling: Balthasar's Negative Theology of Revelation." In *Journal of Religion* 82 (2002) 586–616.

———. "Unapocalyptic Theology: History and Eschatology in Balthasar's Theo-Drama." In *Modern Theology* 17 (2001) 201–25.

Löser, Werner. "Being Interpreted As Love: Reflections on the Theology of Hans Urs von Balthasar." In *Communio* 16 (1989) 475–90.

———. "The Ignatian Exercises in the Work of Hans Urs von Balthasar." In *Hans Urs von Balthasar: His Life and Work*, edited by David L. Schindler, 103–20. San Francisco: Ignatius, 1991.

Louth, Andrew. "The Place of *Heart of the World* in the Theology of Hans Urs von Balthasar." In *The Analogy of Beauty: The Theology of Hans Urs von Balthasar,* edited by John Riches, 147–63. Edinburgh: T&T Clark, 1986.

Mansini, Guy, OSB. "Balthasar and the Theodramatic Enrichment of the Trinity." In *The Thomist* 64 (2000) 499–519.

Martin, Jennifer Newsome. *Hans Urs von Balthasar And the Critical Appropriation of Russian Religious Thought*. Notre Dame, Indiana: University of Notre Dame Press, 2015.

Martin, Ralph. *Will Many Be Saved? What Vatican II Actually Teaches and Its Implications for the New Evangelism*. Grand Rapids, MI: Eerdmans, 2012.

Moss, David, and Edward T. Oakes, SJ. "Introduction." In *The Cambridge Companion to Hans Urs von Balthasar,* edited by Edward T. Oakes, SJ, and David Moss, 1–8. Cambridge: Cambridge University Press, 2004.

Nandkisore, Robert. *Hoffnung auf Erlösung: Die Eschatologie im Werk Hans Urs von Balthasars*. Tesi Gregoriana Serie Teologia No. 22. Rome: Editrice Pontificia Università Gregoriana, 1997.

Nichols, Aidan, OP. *Divine Fruitfulness: A Guide through Balthasar's Theology Beyond the Trilogy*. Washington, DC: The Catholic University of America Press, 2007.

———. *No Bloodless Myth: A Guide Through Balthasar's Dramatics*. Washington DC: The Catholic University of America Press, 2000.

———. *Say it is Pentecost: A Guide Through Balthasar's Logic*. Washington DC: The Catholic University of America Press, 2000.

———. *Scattering the Seed: A Guide through Balthasar's Early Writings on Philosophy and the Arts*. Washington DC: The Catholic University of America Press, 2006.

———. "The Theo-Logic." In *The Cambridge Companion to Hans Urs von Balthasar,* edited by Edward T. Oakes, SJ, and David Moss. Cambridge: Cambridge University Press, 2004.

———. *The Word Has Been Abroad: A Guide Through Balthasar's Aesthetics*. Washington DC: The Catholic University of America Press, 1998.

Nielsen, Philip. "Depicting the Whole Christ: Hans Urs von Balthasar and Sacred Architecture." In *Sacred Architecture* 16 (2009) 30–34.

Oakes, Edward T., SJ. "Hans Urs von Balthasar: The Wave and the Sea." In *Theology Today* 62 (2005) 364–74.

———. "'He Descended into Hell': The Depths of God's Self-Emptying Love on Holy Saturday in the Thought of Hans Urs von Balthasar." In *Exploring Kenotic Christology: The Self-Emptying of God,* edited by C. Stephen Evans, 218–45. Oxford: Oxford University Press, 2006.

———. "The Internal Logic of Holy Saturday in the Theology of Hans Urs von Balthasar." In *International Journal of Systematic Theology* 9 (2007) 184–99.

———. *Pattern of Redemption: The Theology of Hans Urs von Balthasar.* New York: Continuum, 1994.

O'Donaghue, Noel. "A Theology of Beauty." In *The Analogy of Beauty: The Theology of Hans Urs von Balthasar,* edited by John Riches, 1–10. Edinburgh: T&T Clark, 1986.

O'Donnell, John, SJ. "Hans Urs von Balthasar: The Form of His Theology." In *Hans Urs von Balthasar: His Life and Work,* edited by David L. Schindler, 207–20. San Francisco: Ignatius, 1991.

———. "Truth as Love: The Understanding of Truth According to Hans Urs von Balthasar." In *Pacifica* 1 (1988) 189–211.

O'Hanlon, Gerard F. *The Immutability of God in the Theology of Hans Urs von Balthasar.* Cambridge: Cambridge University Press, 1990.

O'Reagan, Cyril. "Balthasar and Gnostic Genealogy." In *Modern Theology* 22 (2006) 609–50.

Oster, Stefan. "The Other and the Fruitfulness of Personal Acting." In *Love Alone is Credible: Hans Urs von Balthasar as Interpreter of the Catholic Tradition,* edited by David L. Schindler, 303–17. Grand Rapids, MI: Eerdmans, 2008.

Ouellet, Marc. "The Message of Balthasar's Theology to Modern Theology." In *Communio* 23 (1996) 270–99.

———. "Paradox and/or Supernatural Existential." In *Communio* 18 (1991) 259–80.

Papanikolaou, Aristotle. "Person, *Kenosis* and Abuse: Hans Urs von Balthasar and Feminist Theologies in Conversation." In *Modern Theology* 19 (2003) 41–65.

Pelikan, Jaroslav. *The Emergence of the Catholic Tradition (100–600).* Chicago: University of Chicago Press, 1971.

Pitstick, Alyssa Lyra. *Light in Darkness: Hans Urs von Balthasar and The Catholic Doctrine of Christ's Descent into Hell.* Grand Rapids, MI: Eerdmans, 2007.

Pitstick, Alyssa Lyra, and Edward T. Oakes, SJ. "Balthasar, Hell and Heresy: An Exchange." In *First Things* 168 (2006) 25–32.

Power, Dermot. "The Holy Saturday Experience." *The Way* 38 (1998) 32–39.

Quash, Ben. "Ignatian Dramatics: First Glance at the Spirituality of Hans Urs von Balthasar." In *The Way* 38 (1998) 77–86.

———. "The Theo-Drama." In *The Cambridge Companion to Hans Urs von Balthasar,* edited by Edward T. Oakes, SJ, and David Moss, 143–57. Cambridge: Cambridge University Press, 2004.

Rahner, Karl. *Foundations of Christian Faith.* Translated by William V. Dych. New York: Seabury, 1978.

———. *On the Theology of Death.* Translated by Charles H. Henkey. New York: Herder and Herder, 1961.

Ratzinger, Joseph. "Christian Universalism: On Two Collections of Papers by Hans Urs von Balthasar." In *Communio* 22 (1995) 545–57.

———. *Eschatology. Death and Eternal Life*. Translated by Aidan Nichols, O.P. Washington DC: The Catholic University of America Press, 1988.

———. "Homily at the Funeral of Hans Urs von Balthasar." In *Hans Urs von Balthasar: His Life and Work*, edited by David L. Schindler, 291–98. San Francisco: Ignatius, 1991.

———. *Introduction to Christianity*. Translated by J.R. Foster. New York: Seabury, 1979.

Riches, John. "Balthasar and the Analysis of Faith." In *The Analogy of Beauty: The Theology of Hans Urs von Balthasar*, edited by John Riches, 35–69. Edinburgh: T&T Clark, 1986.

Roten, Johann S.M. "The Two Halves of the Moon: Marian Anthropological Dimensions in the Common Mission of Adrienne von Speyr and Hans Urs von Balthasar." In *Hans Urs von Balthasar: His Life and Work*, edited by David L. Schindler, 65–86. San Francisco: Ignatius, 1991.

Sachs, John R., SJ. "Current Eschatology: Universal Salvation and the Problem of Hell." In *Theological Studies* 52 (1991) 227–54.

Sara, Juan M. "*Descensus Ad Inferos*, Dawn of Hope: Aspects of the Theology of Holy Saturday in the Trilogy of Hans Urs von Balthasar." In *Communio* 32 (2005) 541–72.

Saward, John. "Mary and Peter in the Christological Constellation: Balthasar's Ecclesiology." In *The Analogy of Beauty: The Theology of Hans Urs von Balthasar*, edited by John Riches, 105–33. Edinburgh: T&T Clark, 1986.

Scola, Angelo. *Hans Urs von Balthasar: A Theological Style*. Grand Rapids, MI: Eerdmans, 1995.

Servais, Jacques. "Balthasar as Interpreter of the Catholic Tradition." In *Love Alone is Credible: Hans Urs von Balthasar as Interpreter of the Catholic Tradition*, edited by David L. Schindler, 191–208. Grand Rapids, MI: Eerdmans, 2008.

———. "Freedom as Christ's Gift to Man in the Thought of Hans Urs von Balthasar." In *Communio* 29 (2002) 556–78.

Schindler, David C. "Towards a Non-Possessive Concept of Knowledge: On the Relation Between Reason and Love in Aquinas and Balthasar." In *Modern Theology* 22 (2006) 577–607.

Schindler, David L. "Modernity and the Nature of a Distinction." In *How Balthasar Changed My Mind*, edited by Rodney A. Howsare and Larry S. Chapp, 224–58. New York: Crossroad, 2008.

Schumacher, Michele M. "The Concept of Representation in the Theology of Hans Urs von Balthasar." In *Theological Studies* 60 (1999) 53–71.

Simon, Ulrich. "Balthasar on Goethe." In *The Analogy of Beauty: The Theology of Hans Urs von Balthasar*, edited by John Riches, 60–76. Edinburgh: T&T Clark, 1986.

von Speyr, Adrienne. *Book of All Saints*. Translated by D.C. Schindler. San Francisco: Ignatius, 2008.

———. *The Christian State of Life*. Translated by Sister Mary Frances McCarthy. San Francisco: Ignatius, 1986.

———. *Confession*. Translated by Douglas W. Stott. San Francisco: Ignatius, 1985.

———. *The Countenance of the Father*. Translated by Dr. David Kipp. San Francisco: Ignatius, 1997.

———. *The Cross & Sacrament*. Translated by Graham Harrison. San Francisco: Ignatius, 1983.

———. *The Gates of Eternal Life*. Translated by Sister Corona Sharp. San Francisco: Ignatius, 1983.

———. *The Letter to the Colossians*. Translated by Michael J. Miller. San Francisco: Ignatius, 1998.

———. *The Letter to the Ephesians*. Translated by Adrian Walker. San Francisco: Ignatius, 1996.

———. *My Early Years*. Edited by Hans Urs von Balthasar. Translated by Mary Emily Hamilton and Dennis D. Martin. San Francisco: Ignatius, 1995.

———. *The Mystery of Death*. Translated by Graham Harrison. San Francisco: Ignatius, 1988.

———. *The Passion From Within*. Translated by Sister Lucia Wiedenhover, OCD. San Francisco: Ignatius, 1998.

Steck, Christopher, SJ. "Tragedy and the Ethics of Hans Urs von Balthasar." In *Annual of the Society of Christian Ethics* 21 (2001) 233–50.

Sutton, Matthew Lewis. "Hans Urs von Balthasar and Adrienne von Speyr's Ecclesial Relationship." In *New Blackfriars* 94 (2012) 50–63.

———. *Heaven Opens: The Trinitarian Mysticism of Adrienne von Speyr*. Minneapolis, MN: Fortress, 2014.

Taylor, Sheila. "The Hope for Universal Salvation." In *Element* 2 (2006) 39–54.

Tourpe, Emmanuel. "Dialectic and Dialogic: The Identity of Being as Fruitfulness in Hans Urs von Balthasar." In *Love Alone is Credible: Hans Urs von Balthasar as Interpreter of the Catholic Tradition*, edited by David L. Schindler, 318–30. Grand Rapids, MI: Eerdmans, 2008.

Turek, Margaret M. "'As the Father Loved Me' (Jn 15:9). Towards a Theology of God the Father: Hans Urs von Balthasar's Theodramatic Approach." PhD diss., University of Fribourg, 1999.

Vasko, Elizabeth T. "Suffering and the Search for Wholeness: Beauty and the Cross in Hans Urs von Balthasar and Contemporary Feminist Theologies." PhD diss., Loyola Chicago University, 2009.

Wainright, Geoffrey. "Eschatology." In *The Cambridge Companion to Hans Urs von Balthasar*, edited by Edward T. Oakes, SJ, and David Moss, 113–30. Cambridge: Cambridge University Press, 2004.

Walker, Adrian J. "Love Alone: Hans Urs von Balthasar as a Master of Theological Renewal." In *Love Alone is Credible: Hans Urs von Balthasar as Interpreter of the Catholic Tradition*, edited by David L. Schindler, 16–40. Grand Rapids, MI: Eerdmans, 2008.

Webster, John. "Balthasar and Karl Barth" in *The Cambridge Companion to Hans Urs von Balthasar*, edited by Edward T. Oakes, SJ and David Moss, 241 -55. Cambridge: Cambridge University Press, 2004.

White, Thomas Joseph, OP. "On the Universal Possibility of Salvation." In *Pro Ecclesia* 17 (2008) 269–80.

Wigley, Stephen. *Balthasar's Trilogy*. New York: Continuum, 2010.

———. "The von Balthaar thesis: a re-examination of von Balthasar's Study of Barth in the Light of Bruce McCormack." In *Scottish Journal of Theology* 56 (2003) 345–59.

Williams, Rowan. "Balthasar and Rahner." In *The Analogy of Beauty: The Theology of Hans Urs von Balthasar*, edited by John Riches, 11–34. Edinburgh: T&T Clark, 1986.

———. "Balthasar and the Trinity." In *The Cambridge Companion to Hans Urs von Balthasar*, edited by Edward T. Oakes, SJ, and David Moss, 37–50. Cambridge: Cambridge University Press, 2004.

Yeago, David S. "Literature in the Drama of Nature and Grace." In *Glory, Grace and Culture: The Work of Hans Urs von Balthasar,* edited by Ed Block Jr., 88–106. New York: Paulist, 2005.

Zaborrowski, Holger. "Mythos oder Geschichte: Hans Urs von Balthasar und die griechische Tragödie." In *Logik der Liebe und Herrlichkeit Gottes: Hans Urs von Balthasar im Gespräch (FS für K. Lehmann)*, edited by Walter Kasper, 45–63. Ostfildern: Mathias Grünewald Verlag, 2006.

46609858R00099

Made in the USA
Middletown, DE
04 August 2017